Taking Charge

An Introduction to Electricity

Larry E. Schafer

◆

A Project of Horizon Research, Inc.

Materials for middle-grade teachers in physical science

This project was funded by BP America, Inc.

The National Science Teachers Association

Produced by Special Publications
National Science Teachers Association
1742 Connecticut Avenue, NW
Washington, DC 20009

Stock Number PB–96
ISBN 0-87355-110-9

TAKING CHARGE

Table of Contents

MODULE 2

Current Electricity

81

◆Acknowledgements

A project like *Taking Charge: An Introduction to Electricity* does not reach publication without the contributions and enthusiastic support of many people. Foremost among these are Norman Anderson, Jack Wheatley, and Karen Johnston of North Carolina State University who developed the original concept for this volume. Ann C. Howe, formerly of NCSU, was project co-director, along with Iris R. Weiss of Horizon Research, Inc.

Teachers who shared their experience to create this project include Laureen Andrews, Annette Bingham, Shirley Blanks, Bill Boudman, Cleopatra Carr, Linda Poore, William Crews, Linda Hicks, Betty Sturdivant, Bennie Mims, Elaine Nagle, and Jane Smith.

Larry Schafer of Syracuse University built upon the work of these people to write the book you see before you. Special gratitude goes to Dr. Schafer for his creativity, hard work, patience, and appreciation of critical reviews. The manuscript was carefully reviewed by Judith Bodnick of Milton Academy, Milton, MA; Robert Starr of SUNY, Plattsburgh; Patricia Rourke of St. Agnes School, Alexandria, VA; and Ron Morris of East Syracuse-Minoa High School, East Syracuse, NY. Our appreciation also goes to Mario Iona, professor emeritus of Physics at the University of Denver, for making many useful comments.

Sondra Hardis of BP America, Inc. provided valuable suggestions for disseminating this material, helping to establish links between it and many potential users. Phyllis Marcuccio of the National Science Teachers Association handled the arrangements that made production of this book possible.

Taking Charge was produced by NSTA Special Publications, Shirley Watt Ireton, managing editor; Andrew Saindon, associate editor; Christine Pearce, associate editor; Daniel Shannon, editorial assistant. Andrew Saindon was NSTA project editor for this book. At AURAS Design, the book was designed by Sharon H. Wolfgang; the art director for the cover was Rob Sugar. Special thanks go to Brian Marquis for cover ideas. Illustrations were created by Max-Karl Winkler and Larry Schafer. Circuit diagrams were created by Andrew Saindon, from originals by Larry Schafer. The illustration on page 103 is by Sergey Ivanov. The contributions of all these people were essential in the preparation of this book.

Taking Charge was a project of Horizon Research, Inc. Project Director was Iris R. Weiss; project co-director was Ann C. Howe.

Special thanks go to BP America, Inc., for providing the funds to make this project possible.

OVERVIEW

Taking Charge
An Introduction to Electricity

Only a few hundred years ago, Ben Franklin wondered whether the lightning which divided the thundering blackness was the same phenomenon as the sparks he observed in his electrical experiments. From those early investigations, we have progressed in our knowledge of electricity to a point where today we can create a computer so fast that it can "read" the entire Library of Congress in seconds. While electrical technology continues to rapidly develop and work its way into our everyday lives (computers, fax machines), most of us thrash about with vague and primitive notions about even the simplest electrical phenomena. The purpose of this book is to provide you, the teacher, with a resource of activities which can be used in helping learners acquire a basic understanding of simple electrical phenomena. Although the book includes explanations for how certain products reduce static cling, how photocopy machines work, and how electricity could add a little zap to a good night kiss, the emphasis is on understanding simple "everyday" electrical events.

◆Organization of this book

The book is divided into two modules: one on static electricity and one on current electricity. The static electricity module is organized around a historical perspective. The primary purpose of this historical perspective is to help learners understand the nature of science—that science is not a set of correct, never-changing truths but that it is a process through which people create, judge, and re-create ideas in light of observations, evidence, and argument. You might be concerned that the introduction of history will unnecessarily expose students to incorrect ideas. Although both Ben Franklin and Charles Dufay's ideas about electricity were not entirely correct and complete, both men created ideas which are consistent with the modern view of static electricity. In other words, after learning of the ideas of Franklin and Dufay, students do not have to discard those ideas, but have to weave them together to develop the more modern conception of static electricity.

The static electricity module is presented before the current electricity module. However, static electricity need not be covered before students engage in many of the current electricity activities. Much of current electricity is concrete and more easily understood than some of the ideas presented in static electricity.

Each student activity includes an introduction, a description of materials needed, a statement of objectives, and procedures to follow. None of the activities require "high tech" equipment such as electrical meters. Almost all of the materials, with perhaps the exception of Fahnestock clips and sockets for flashlight bulbs, can be acquired locally. The objectives are general descriptions of what will happen in the activity and are not precise statements of what students will learn from the activity.

The procedure section is designed so that students can perform the activity without your constant involvement and direction. This section presents students with problems they are to solve with the designated materials, provides questions for students to answer, and provides spaces for students to record their observations and answers. Wherever possible and appropriate, students are challenged with problems to solve. The problem might be solved through the manipulation of materials (Design a two bulb circuit so that when one bulb is unscrewed from the socket, the other bulb goes out) or through the application of ideas (When your finger touched and discharged the electroscope, which way did electrons flow?). It should be clear that these activities require substantive student thought. Underlying the design of these activities is the idea that students will meaningfully understand as a consequence of figuring things out for themselves. Students should be encouraged as they struggle and rewarded for their thinking, creativity, and persistence.

Each activity is accompanied by a guide to the activity. The guide is written for you and includes an overview of what will happen in the activity, directions for the construction of equipment or the selection of materials, time management recommendations, cautionary notes, answers to the questions, and ideas for extended activities.

◆Getting ready for classroom instruction

The activities in each of the modules are sequenced so that students participating in any given activity have the experience and knowledge they need from the previous activities to complete that given activity. However, this does not mean that students have to complete all of the previous activities prior to engaging in any given activity. Nor does it mean that you could or should use all of these activities. You are encouraged to be creative and flexible with these materials. You might not use any of the activities as presented, but read through the activities searching for ideas, activities, problems, equipment, and explanations which might be of use in your classroom.

Many of the activities in both modules are appropriate for younger students (grades 5 and 6). However, you need to assess the ability of your younger students before introducing some of the more involved activities. For example, fifth grade students will be able to solve many of the current electricity problems; however, fifth graders will likely have difficulty with the series of activities that develop Ohm's Law. A number of the static electricity activities require students to keep track of and trace the movement of charges. These activities will challenge the patience and thinking ability of younger students and should be modified for or not used at all with younger students.

Static electricity activities are notoriously troublesome. A particularly humid day can make a liar out of even the most upright and concientious teacher. During the development of these activities, there was a constant search for materials and procedures which produced consistent results regardless of weather conditions. The search resulted in improving the reliability of many of the static electricity activities. There is, however, no absolute guarantee that each activity will work flawlessly without some "patient fiddling." A key to the success of many of the activities is the use of Plexiglas strips. Whereas silk-rubbed glass is often suggested as a source of positive charge, silk-rubbed Plexiglas seems to produce a stronger and more persistent positive charge. Not all "plastics" produce a persistent charge. Since success has been found with Plexiglas, we suggest that you take the extra time to locate genuine Plexiglas for use in the activities.

Some of the later activities rely on materials and procedures described in earlier activities. If you do not implement the earlier activities, it might prove helpful for you to read the relevant sections from the earlier activities.

There is a tendency in some students to investigate on their own in backyards and basements. While you should encourage this, investigations can be particularly dangerous if they are attempts to repeat Ben Franklin's lightning demonstrations or if they are investigations that involve household electricity. It is vitally important for you to make students comfortable with the harmless activities in this book while at the same time warning students against any attempt to investigate lightning and household electricity.

This book is offered to help you and your students engage in challenging activities which lead to a meaningful understanding of basic electrical phenomena. The emphasis is on creating a depth of understanding. This book sets the stage for the study of electromagnetism, electrical power generation, and electronics.

MODULE 1

Static Electricity

◆Introduction

•Why do rubbed balloons stick to walls?

•How can a charged object attract uncharged objects?

•How do photocopiers work?

Answering these questions requires using the principles of electrostatics. It requires an understanding of the structure of the atom and the interaction of charged particles and objects.

The activities in Module 1 provide an introduction to the ideas of early explorers like Ben Franklin to show how we developed our modern view of electricity. The activities also provide practice in designing experiments, visualizing the placement of static charges, and observing the behavior of charged and uncharged objects.

◆Instructional Objectives

After completing the activities for Module 1, you should be able to

• identify what is "static" about electrostatic attraction and repulsion [Activities 1, 2, and 3]

• determine how early observations of electricity shaped our modern ideas [Activities 4, 5, 6, 7, and 8]

• determine how electrical charges move within some objects and sometimes between objects [Activities 9, 10, 11, and 12]

• answer the question "Why are uncharged objects attracted to charged objects?" [Activity 13]

• identify the roles static electricity plays in our lives [Activity 14]

ACTIVITY 1 WORKSHEET

Tree Sap—How Attractive!

Part 1

◆Background

To move an object at rest, you must pull it or push it . . . but do you have to touch it?

◆Objective

To find one way of getting objects to move without touching them

◆Procedure

1. Set the paper cylinder on a flat surface. Make sure the cylinder can easily roll when you give it a gentle push.

2. **Challenge:** Get the cylinder to roll a distance of one meter without allowing any object (you, air, breath, spit ball, etc.) to touch it. You cannot tip the table nor can you change the cylinder in any way. You can use only the strip of Plexiglas™, silk, flannel, and metal spoon.

3. Describe in writing or with pictures how you solved the problem:

4. What material(s) make the cylinder move?

_____

_____

5. You have just investigated one kind of non-touching interaction or interaction-at-a-distance. There are other kinds of interactions-at-a-distance. The Earth does not have to touch you to exert a pull on you. To convince yourself of this, think of jumping off your chair to the floor. While you are in mid air, not touching the floor or the Earth, the Earth is pulling you down. This pull is called gravitational interaction.

If you bring a magnet near a paper clip, the paper clip moves towards the magnet without the magnet touching it. This is called magnetic interaction. In this activity, the cylinder rolled without an object touching it. This is called electrical interaction.

Materials

For each group:
Part 1
• a metal spoon
• a piece of silk cloth
• a piece of flannel
• a strip of Plexiglas™
• a cylinder of paper (about a 3 cm x 20 cm strip rolled into a 6 cm diameter cylinder or hoop)
• a meter stick

Part 2
• a wooden pencil
• a piece of chalk
• a large metal paper clip
• a small inflated balloon
• a small piece of facial tissue
• a quarter
• a small piece of aluminum foil

Part 2

◆Background

What does tree sap have to do with this activity? You discovered that you could rub a strip of Plexiglas with silk and use the rubbed strip of Plexiglas to move a cylinder of paper without touching the cylinder.

The ancient Greeks rubbed a yellowish-brown material called amber and observed that it attracted small bits of straw and other materials without touching them. We now know that amber is the fossilized sap, or resin, from trees that lived millions of years ago. The Greek word for amber is *electron*—from which we get the term electricity. The study of electricity started many years ago when it was discovered that rubbed tree sap (the old, hardened variety) would attract small bits of certain materials.

It wasn't until the 1570s that William Gilbert started to carefully investigate which materials could be "electrified" and which could not. He called those rubbed materials that attracted small bits of materials "electrics." He called those materials which could *not* be electrified "non-electrics." This scientist was the court physician to Queen Elizabeth I of England and also was the first person to realize that the Earth acted like a large magnet.

◆Objective

To discover which materials can be used to produce this "non-touching" push or pull and which cannot

◆Procedure

Using the materials from Part 1 and Part 2—

6. **Challenge:** Carry on Gilbert's investigation to discover which rubbed materials are electrics (can attract bits of paper) and which are non-electrics.

7. Cut the facial tissue so that you have 5–10 small pieces (about 0.5 cm square or 1/4 the size of your fingernail).

8. Rub the objects with flannel and hold them close to the small bits of tissue, noting which rubbed materials can be electrified (made attractive).

9. Record your observations by circling "electric" or "non-electric" on the chart on the next page.

10. Let's say you continued to test materials and found that the following items were non-electrics: gold ring, steel dog chain, brass knuckles, horseshoe, and the wire used in braces for teeth. Based on your data from the chart and this list, what could you conclude about some of the materials which are non-electrics?

_____

_____

Data chart

Material Rubbed With Flannel	Circle One	
a. Strip of Plexiglas	Electric	Non-Electric
b. Paper Clip (metal)	Electric	Non-Electric
c. Wooden Pencil	Electric	Non-Electric
d. Metal Spoon	Electric	Non-Electric
e. Inflated Balloon	Electric	Non-Electric
f. Chalk	Electric	Non-Electric
g. Aluminum foil	Electric	Non-Electric
h. Quarter	Electric	Non-Electric
Other Materials		
i. _____	Electric	Non-Electric
j. _____	Electric	Non-Electric

11. Based on your data, could you say that all non-metals are electrics? Explain your answer.

_____

_____

_____

_____

12. Cut or tear aluminum foil so that you have 5–10 small pieces (about 0.5 cm square or 1/4 the size of your fingernail). Do you think a rubbed electric will attract the bits of foil?

_____

13. Rub the balloon (an electric) with flannel and see if it attracts the bits of foil. Was the foil attracted?

_____

Were you "foiled?"

GUIDE TO ACTIVITY 1

Tree Sap—How Attractive!

◆What is happening?

In this activity, students duplicate some historical investigations of electricity. As in the those early investigations, the focus is on electrical attraction and on the identification of materials which can and cannot be electrified by rubbing. In solving the first problem, students will discover that a strip of Plexiglas rubbed with silk will move the paper cylinder without touching it. As the strip of Plexiglas moves, the paper cylinder will roll along behind it. During subsequent parts of this activity the students will discover the following.

• Some rubbed objects attract small, light bits of materials.
• The ability to attract (electrification) goes away after a while and the object must be rubbed again before it regains its ability to attract.
• If a metal is held in the hand (such as the spoon in this activity) and rubbed, it will not be electrified by rubbing. If, on the other hand, the metal is supported by a material called an insulator (glass, resin, plastic) and rubbed, the rubbed metal will become electrified. In later activities, students will observe that insulated metals can be electrified. In the early 1700s, an English electrician named Stephen Gray was the first to demonstrate that rubbed metals resting on blocks of resin (an insulator) could be electrified.
• Some non-metals can be electrified by rubbing and therefore are identified as electrics. A strip of Plexiglas and a rubber balloon can be rubbed with material to produce a rather strong attraction. Some non-metals are not good electrics (chalk, wood, etc.).
• Both non-metals (small pieces of tissue) and metals (small pieces of aluminum foil) can be attracted to an electrified object. The students might find this perplexing. If you cannot rub a metal to electrify it, how can a metal be attracted to some electrified object?

In this activity we will show that certain rubbed materials can attract small, light bits of material. We will not explain why the attraction takes place. This explanation will come later after students have developed the ideas necessary for understanding the explanation. See Activity 13 for the explanation.

◆Time management

One class period (40–60 minutes) should provide enough time to complete this activity. Or you could complete Parts 1 and 2 in separate periods, using the ideas in "Suggestions for further study" to round out each period.

◆Preparation

Static electricity experiments and demonstrations are best done on days when the humidity is low. Although many of these activities will work on humid days, it's best to test out the materials and effects before presenting the activities to students.

The selection of materials used in static electricity activities is crucial. Some rubbed materials produce a strong electrical effect while others, which appear to have the same properties, produce very little electrical effect. The materials used in traditional static electricity activities are glass and hard rubber rods and silk and wool cloth or fur. There are other materials which are easily acquired and often produce very strong electrical effects.

Strips of Plexiglas—When Plexiglas is rubbed with silk, a rather strong and persistent positive charge is produced on the Plexiglas. Plexiglas can be purchased in sheets from hardware stores. Some stores have irregular or scratched pieces which they will sell at a bargain. The sheets can be cut into strips which are approximately 22 cm long, 3 cm wide, and 0.3 cm thick. Plexiglas can be sawed, or scored and broken like glass. Use a utility knife to score (deeply scratch) the plastic. Break over a straight edge which lies along the score. Sand the edges and corners of the strips.

Other materials that can be electrified are:

• Rolled overhead transparency—Some transparencies will acquire a strong charge when rubbed with silk cloth. To make a rolled overhead transparency, simply roll a sheet lengthwise and tape it at both ends and the middle with transparent tape. The roll should be about 2 cm in diameter and about 27–28 cm long. Not all overhead transparency material can be easily electrified. Test one before obtaining classroom quantities.

• Cassette tape boxes—Clear plastic cassette tape boxes acquire a charge when rubbed with silk.

• Inflated rubber balloons—When inflated balloons are rubbed with flannel, they acquire a charge. For this activity purchase small, inexpensive balloons.

• Silk and flannel—There are many materials which are not silk but look like silk. If you are not sure, purchase the cheapest (and perhaps the ugliest) silk you can from a fabric store. Cotton or wool flannel should be easier to identify. The squares of cloth should be about 15 cm on a side.

• Paper cylinder—Cut 2.5–3.0 cm x 21.5 cm strips from the short side of a regular sheet of paper. Roll each strip to form a cylinder which is about 6 cm in diameter. Use a very small amount of transparent tape or glue to connect the ends of the strip. The cylinder should not be too "bottom heavy" where the ends are connected; otherwise the cylinder will not easily roll.

◆Suggestions for further study

Casting a spell on the witch's broom—Challenge students to come up with a way of getting a broomstick to move or twirl around without the motion being caused by anything touching the stick. The students can only use a soda bottle lid, a piece of flannel cloth, and a large balloon.

The solution: If the broomstick is balanced on the soda bottle lid, which has its top and smooth side down on a smooth surface, the broom handle can be easily twirled. The charge on a balloon rubbed with flannel

is enough to start and sustain the twirling action without the balloon touching the handle. Any long piece of wood (125 cm x 2 cm x 1.5 cm) or a metal rod can be substituted for the broom handle.

Challenge students to bring in objects to test as electrics or non-electrics. Challenge students to find evidence which is contrary to the conclusion that metals are non-electrics (cannot be electrified to attract small bits of materials).

In Activity 1, small bits of paper and aluminum foil were used to determine if a rubbed object was electrified. What other small, light materials might be attracted to electrified objects? Ground coffee, instant coffee (freeze dried), gelatin, puffed breakfast cereals, pepper, hair, and pieces of Styrofoam are among the many materials that are attracted by electrified objects. How would students argue against the explanation that freeze dried instant coffee is attracted to rubbed objects because the once frozen coffee is trying to warm up?

◆Answers

3. and 4. A silk-rubbed piece of Plexiglas will attract and roll the cylinder without touching it.

9. a. electric   b. non-electric c. non-electric d. non-electric e. electric
f. non-electric g. non-electric h. non-electric
i. _____ j. _____

10. Metals (spoon and paper clip) are non-electrics.

11. No. Wood is a non-metal and is a non-electric.

12. Answers vary.

13. Yes. Answers vary. The foil bits are attracted. Tell students that at a later time they will learn how non-electric objects (foil bits) are attracted to an electrified object.

ACTIVITY 2 WORKSHEET

So Where's the Attraction? What's Static about Static Electricity?

◆Background

The phrase "static electricity" is used in describing a number of situations:
• the "snap, crackle, and zing" that occurs when you pull off your sweater from over your shirt or blouse
• the little zap you get when you touch a light switch after walking across a carpet
• clothing that sticks together just after being removed from the drier
• the rubbed balloon or strip of Plexiglas that attracts small bits of paper

We are dealing with electricity in these situations. In other activities we will learn more about what electricity is. In this activity we will focus on what we mean by "static."

◆Objectives

To discover what is "static" about static electricity

◆Procedure

1. If the balloon is not marked, use the marker to make three lines, evenly spaced around the balloon (see diagram at left). The lines should be at least 3 cm apart. Number the lines 1, 2, and 3. If a balloon is already marked, use that balloon.

2. Tear the tissue into 5–10 pieces about 1/4 the size of your fingernail.

3. After the marks have dried on the balloon, give the marked balloon and the flannel cloth to one member of the group. Without other group members seeing, the student with the balloon rubs the flannel back and forth along *only one* of the three lines.

Be sure to handle the balloon only by the knot when rubbing. Give the balloon back to the other group members, who are challenged to use the materials to discover which line was rubbed.

4. Describe in writing and/or with drawings the method that you used for identifying the rubbed line.

Materials

For each group:
• one small, inflated balloon
• a piece of flannel cloth
• a small piece of facial tissue or toilet paper
• a marker

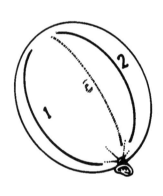

5. Why do you believe—or don't you believe—that the electrical influence (area of attraction) spreads around on the balloon that was rubbed?

_____

_____

6. Look up the word "static" in the dictionary. Describe what you think is meant by "static electricity."

_____

_____

GUIDE TO ACTIVITY 2

So Where's the Attraction? What's Static about Static Electricity?

◆What is happening?

In this activity, students should discover that:

Only the rubbed area (the chosen line on the balloon) attracts small bits of tissue paper. The electrical influence or area of attraction does not spread around the object to those areas which have not been rubbed. Therefore, because the electricity does not move around, we call it static electricity.

There is a change, however: the electrical influence eventually decreases and goes away. In Activity 11 we will show how static electricity can be turned into current (moving) electricity—what we use to power light bulbs, radios, and other devices.

◆Time management

One class period (40–60 minutes) should be enough time to complete the activity and discuss the results.

◆Preparation

Use small, inexpensive balloons. Balloons salvaged from the first activity can be used in this activity.

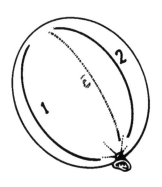

Use markers which produce lines on the balloon that are not easily rubbed off. If enough markers are not available, mark one balloon for each group. The marks should be 8–10 cm long and evenly spaced around the balloon, at least 3 cm apart. Number the lines from 1 to 3.

Use ordinary facial tissue or toilet paper. Check the static attraction of any tissue that has lotion added to it.

Use the 15-cm-square pieces of flannel from Activity 1.

Before beginning this activity make sure that the balloons are not electrified. Also, caution the students at the beginning of the lesson to rub the balloons only where they are told and to hold the balloons by the knot when rubbing. The first part of the activity will not work if all parts of the balloons are electrified.

If the humidity is low and the balloons remain electrified for a long time, this activity could be modified by giving each group a partially electrified balloon and the challenge of finding the area (or areas) of the balloon that is electrified.

◆Suggestions for further study

Challenge students to see how long it takes for static electricity to go away on the balloon.

What can students do to remove static electricity from a balloon?

Challenge students to find other objects that can be electrified and rub only one part of the object to see if bits of paper are attracted only to that rubbed area.

◆Answers

4.   If the balloon is held close to a pile of small pieces of tissue and the balloon is slowly twirled around, the balloon will pick up tissue only where it has been rubbed.

5. The electrical influence does not move around on the object. Only that area which is rubbed is electrified.

   Note: Students might find some electrified areas (areas which attract tissue) which have not been rubbed by the designated student. This will occur if the balloon has been rubbed by some other means—rubbed accidentally on someone's shirt or rubbed by someone from a previous class period. Sometimes it is necessary to wipe a balloon with a damp cloth to remove the charge from the balloon's surface.

6. Because "static" means "stationary" or "not moving" and because the electrified areas did not move, static electricity must be electricity that does not move around.

ACTIVITY 3 WORKSHEET

Electricity—Can It Be Repulsive?

◆Background

The very early investigators of static electricity observed that some rubbed objects attract small bits of material. We know that an electrified object can attract other objects. Can electrified objects push away from or repel one another?

◆Objectives

To explore the possibility of static repulsion

◆Procedure

1. Tie a balloon at each end of the string. Hold the string in the middle so that the two balloons hang down. If the balloons are doing something, describe what is happening.

_____

_____

2. Rub both balloons *all over* with the flannel cloth. Hold the middle of the string connecting the balloons. Allow the balloons to hang side-by-side and observe how they influence each other. Are the balloons attracting each other or repelling each other?

_____

3. Let's assume for a moment that there are different kinds of electricity. You might get one kind of electricity if you rub one material and you might get a different kind of electricity if you rub a different material. In other words, the material, and what it is rubbed with, might determine the kind of electricity produced.

Based on this assumption, would you conclude that the kind of electricity on the balloons is the same or different?_____ Why?

_____

_____

_____

4. Which statement best describes what you think is true?
a. Objects with the same kind of electricity attract.
b. Objects with the same kind of electricity repel.

Materials

For each group:
• two small, inflated balloons
• one piece of string, about 60 cm long
• piece of flannel cloth

5. If it is true, that objects with the same kind of electricity repel, what might you say about electrified objects which attract?

_____

_____

_____

_____

GUIDE TO ACTIVITY 3

Electricity—Can It Be Repulsive?

◆What is happening?

In this activity, students should discover:

When objects (balloons) made of the same kind of material (rubber) are rubbed by the same material (flannel), they likely acquire the same kind of electricity (assuming there are different kinds of electricity). These objects which have the same kind of electricity repel one another. So far we have not proven that there are different kinds of electricity nor have we proven that different kinds of electricity attract.

◆Time management

This activity as written might take less than one class period (40–60 minutes). See "Suggestions for further study" for related activities and demonstrations.

◆Preparation

Use small, inexpensive balloons here. Make sure that the two balloons for each group are about the same size. Balloons salvaged from the first activities can be used in this activity.

◆Suggestions for further study

Challenge students to provide other evidence that the same kind of materials electrified in the same way repel one another (for example, strands of wool yarn rubbed on a balloon will repel one another).

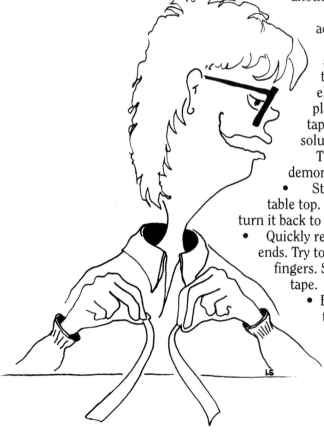

The sticky tape problem (demonstration or activity): Tell the students they will be given two 10-cm strips of transparent tape. Challenge the students to plan a way of using the strips of tape to show that objects with the same kind of electricity repel one another. Once reasonable plans are proposed, give the students the pieces of tape and allow them to implement their plans. One solution is detailed below.

The sticky tape can also be used in either a demonstration or a small group activity:

• Stick two 10-cm pieces of transparent tape to the table top. Leave the "outside" end of each piece free, and turn it back to keep it from sticking to the table.

• Quickly remove the tape strips by pulling on the free ends. Try to prevent the strips from curling around your fingers. Stripping the tape from the table electrifies the tape.

• Bring the two strips of tape close together with the non-sticky sides facing each other. The tapes should repel one another. Because both tapes are made of the same materials and acquired their electrical property by interacting with the same other material (the table), they likely acquired the same kind of electricity. We can conclude that objects with the same kind of electricity repel one another.

◆Answers

1. If the balloons are not electrified, they should touch one another as they hang side by side. If balloons are electrified only in a few areas, they will spin so the electrified areas are away from each other. The balloons will still probably touch.

2. Balloons that have been rubbed all over will repel one another, remaining apart while hanging from the ends of the strings.

3. The kind of electricity on the balloons is the same. Because the same materials (rubber balloons) are electrified in the same way (rubbed with flannel), they should have the same kind of electricity. Objects with the same kind of electricity repel one another.

4. Answer "b" is correct. Objects with the same kind of electricity repel.

5. Correct answers may vary. Based on previous knowledge (opposites attract), a number of students will likely answer that objects with different kinds of electricity (opposites) attract. Some students might base their answer only on what they have seen in the activities and conclude that electrified objects attract objects that are not electrified.

ACTIVITY 4 WORKSHEET

Two Kinds of Electricity or One? Doctor Dufay's Answer!

◆Background

So far you have observed that objects with the same kind of electricity repel and that small, light objects (bits of paper or tissue) which do not appear to be electrified are attracted to electrified objects. You do not know if those small, light objects are electrified. Therefore, you have no evidence that electrified objects can attract each other. If you do observe electrified objects attracting each other, then you might be able to conclude that there are different kinds of electricity.

In this activity, you will see if there is evidence of electrified objects attracting one another and you will learn about Doctor Dufay's ideas about electricity—two kinds of electricity or one?

◆Objectives

To see if electrified objects can attract one another
To infer from observations whether there are different kinds of electricity

◆Procedure

1. Set up the foil flag and ruler on the edge of a table as shown below. Handle the nylon thread as little as possible by touching it only at the end which is attached to the ruler. Make sure the foil flag can freely move and keep the flag as far as possible from the table.

2. Rub the balloon with flannel and move the balloon slowly toward the foil flag. You should see the flag move to the balloon and stick to it.

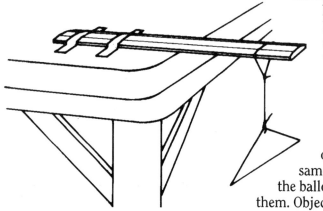

Slowly move the balloon away from the flag, rub the balloon again with flannel, and move the balloon back toward the flag. Repeat this again and again until you see the flag fly away and stay away from the balloon.

When the flag flies away and stays away from the electrified balloon, the flag must have the same kind of electricity as the balloon. You can make this conclusion because in an earlier activity you saw that two electrified balloons repelled each other. Because the two balloons were made of the same materials and rubbed with the same materials, the balloons likely had the same kind of electricity on them. Objects with the same kind of electricity tend to repel.

3. Rub the Plexiglas with silk and try to get the foil flag to fly away and stay away from the electrified Plexiglas. When this happens, the flag should have the same kind of electricity as the Plexiglas.

Experiment until you are sure you know how to get either balloon electricity or Plexiglas electricity on the flag.

4. Use a flannel-rubbed balloon to get balloon electricity on the flag. (The flag is repelled by an electrified balloon.)

When the flag has balloon electricity, move the balloon away. Rub the

Materials

For each group:

• a small foil flag tied to the end of a 30-cm piece of nylon thread

• a plastic ruler or a piece of material (cardboard, stick) similar in size to a ruler

• a small, inflated balloon

• a strip of Plexiglas

• flannel cloth

• silk cloth

• tape

Plexiglas with silk and slowly move the electrified Plexiglas toward the flag. Watch for the *first* movement of the flag.

a. What happens? The flag with balloon electricity first moves (toward, away from)_____ the electrified Plexiglas.

b. Is balloon electricity (on the flag) the same as Plexiglas electricity? Explain your answer:

_____

_____

_____

c. Can electrified objects attract? _____

5. Use a silk-rubbed piece of Plexiglas to get Plexiglas electricity on the flag. (The flag is repelled by an electrified piece of Plexiglas.)

When the flag has Plexiglas electricity, move the Plexiglas away. Rub the balloon with flannel and slowly move the electrified balloon toward the flag. Watch for the *first* movement of the flag.

a. What happens? The flag with Plexiglas electricity first moves (toward, away from)_____ the electrified balloon.

b. Is Plexiglas electricity (on the flag) the same as balloon electricity?_____

c. Does this show that electrified objects might attract? _____

6. You have concluded that balloon electricity and Plexiglas electricity are not the same because objects with these kinds of electricity do not repel. You have also likely observed that electrified objects can attract. All this, however, does not allow you to confidently conclude that different kinds of electricity attract. Why not? Because the electrified flag would have been attracted to the electrified balloon or Plexiglas even if the flag was not electrified. Therefore, the attraction might not be because the flag was electrified. Recall that an electrified object (say, a rubbed balloon) can attract objects which are not electrified (small bits of paper). At this point, you might believe that different kinds of electricity attract, but there is not enough evidence to be sure.

7. If you believe that there are two kinds of electricity (balloon and Plexiglas), you would not be alone. In 1733 a French chemist named Charles Dufay performed investigations similar to the ones above. Instead of using foil flags, Plexiglas, and balloons, he used a very small piece of cork, glass, and resin or amber (hardened tree sap).

Dufay's Views

Doctor Dufay concluded that there are two kinds of electricity: resinous (resin) electricity and vitreous (from a Latin name for glass) electricity.

Doctor Dufay's resin and glass electricity correspond to your balloon and Plexiglas electricity.

Doctor Dufay concluded that the same kinds of electricity repel (resin repels resin and glass repels glass) and that opposite kinds of electricity attract (resin and glass attract).

You will soon learn that Ben Franklin thought that Dufay's ideas were full of tree sap—wrong! Who was right, Dufay or Franklin? We'll see.

GUIDE TO ACTIVITY 4

Two Kinds of Electricity or One? Doctor Dufay's Answer!

◆What is happening?

In the previous activity, we showed that objects with the same kind of electricity repel one another. We have also shown that electrified objects can attract small bits of material. However, because we do not know if those bits of materials are electrified, we cannot conclude that electrified objects attract.

In this activity we show that electrified objects can attract one another. This leads to the possibility that there are two kinds of electricity and that those two kinds attract one another (Doctor Dufay's idea).

Although it is possible that different kinds of electricity attract, this activity does not provide conclusive evidence of the fact. For an explanation, see step 6 in the activity.

◆Time management

One class period (40–60 minutes) should be enough time to complete the activity and discuss the results.

If you think that students might have trouble following directions, hand out the worksheet without the materials and have the students follow you as you demonstrate step 2. After the demonstration, pass out the materials and have the students perform step 2 for themselves before continuing with the remaining steps.

◆Preparation

In this activity you can use the strips of Plexiglas, balloons, and pieces of cloth from Activity 1.

Make the triangular foil flag out of ordinary weight—not heavy duty—aluminum foil. For each flag cut a square of foil about 2.5 cm on a side. Fold the square along the diagonal to make a triangle. Use a pin to put a hole in one of the corners. Thread one end of a 30-cm-length of nylon thread through the hole and gently tie the thread to the flag. Be careful not to tie the thread so tightly that it rips through the flag. Make a large overhand loop at the other end of the string. This loop will slide over the end of the ruler or stick.

These flags are delicate; ask the students to treat them gently. For future use and to avoid tangles, store each flag and its string in a plastic sandwich bag.

Nylon thread, although a good insulator, can be unruly and hard to work with. You might want to try other kinds of string or thread. Just make sure that the flag can stay charged for a reasonable length of time.

◆Suggestions for further study

In this activity students are able to electrify the flag with balloon electricity (flag flies away from an electrified balloon) and they are able to electrify the flag with Plexiglas electricity (flag flies away from an electrified strip of Plexiglas). Have the students give the flag either balloon or Plexiglas electricity and then have them see what other rubbed objects (hard rubber combs, cassette tape boxes, glass, etc.) repel the flag and therefore have the same kind of electricity as the flag. Have students make a list of rubbed objects which have balloon electricity and a list which have Plexiglas electricity.

Make sure the students also record the kind of materials used in rubbing. Also, ask the students to find an answer to the question: If you rub an object with different materials, does the object always acquire the same kind of electricity? (Answer: Not necessarily)

You may wish for students to be more systematic. Have them test all objects rubbed with the same material and then have them repeat the test by rubbing all objects with a different material.

◆Answers

4a. The flag with balloon electricity first moves <u>toward</u> the electrified Plexiglas.

b. The answer is "no." Because objects with the same kind of electricity repel and because these objects attract, balloon electricity cannot be the same as Plexiglas electricity.

c. The answer is "yes." Electrified objects can attract.

5a. The flag with Plexiglas electricity first moves <u>toward</u> the electrified balloon.

b. The answer is "no." Because objects with the same kind of electricity repel and because these objects attract, Plexiglas electricity cannot be the same as balloon electricity.

c. The answer is "yes." Electrified objects can attract.

ACTIVITY 5 WORKSHEET

Two Kinds of Electricity or One? Ben Franklin's Answer!

◆Background

You know that objects with the same kind of electricity repel one another. In the last activity you discovered that two electrified objects can be attracted to each other. These observations led Dr. Dufay to conclude that there are two kinds of electricity. Objects with the same kind of electricity repel and objects with different kinds of electricity attract.

In this activity you will make one of the observations that led Ben Franklin to doubt Dufay's ideas and to create a different idea.

◆Objective

To investigate the electricity on a rubbed object and on the material that was used to rub the object

To understand how the results of this investigation led Ben Franklin to create a new idea about the kinds of electricity

◆Procedure

1. Hang the foil flag on its nylon thread from the ruler as shown below.

2. Give the flag balloon electricity using the same procedure you used in the last activity: Rub the balloon with flannel and touch the electrified balloon to the flag until the flag is repelled by the balloon.

3. With the balloon electricity on the flag, rub the strip of Plexiglas with silk. Immediately, but slowly, move the *silk* toward the electrified flag. Do not allow the flag and silk to touch. What first happens to the flag? The flag is (attracted to, repelled by)

_____ the silk.

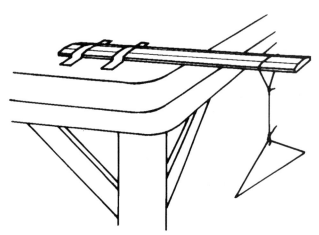

4. With balloon electricity still on the flag (if it is not, repeat step 2), slowly move the electrified strip of Plexiglas toward the electrified flag. What first happens to the flag? The flag is (attracted to, repelled by) _____ the electrified Plexiglas.

5. Look at your answer to step 3. Remember that the flag had balloon electricity and that objects with the same kind of electricity repel. Does the silk have balloon electricity?_____

6. Look at your answer to step 4. Does the electrified Plexiglas have balloon electricity?_____

7. Based on what you concluded in steps 5 and 6, do the Plexiglas and the silk used to rub it have the same kind of electricity?_____

Materials

For each group:
• a foil flag on nylon string
• a ruler or stick about 30 cm long
• a balloon
• a strip of Plexiglas
• flannel cloth
• silk cloth

8. Try creating a general statement. When an object is electrified by being rubbed with a material, the object acquires one kind of electricity and the material acquires:

a. no electricity

b. the same kind of electricity

c. a different kind of electricity

9. Ben Franklin made observations similar to the ones you have just made. He observed that the rubbed object and the material used in rubbing acquired "different kinds" of electricity. He, like you, must have asked himself, why is rubbing necessary to produce electricity and why do the rubbed object and the cloth used in rubbing acquire "different kinds" of electricity?

Franklin also observed that different kinds of electricity could cancel each other out. That is, when an object acquired one kind of electricity and then immediately acquired a different kind of electricity, the object could end up with no electricity. This seemed strange to Franklin. How could you add two different things to the same object and come up with nothing? This would be like adding oranges and apples to the same bag and finding the bag empty.

These observations and questions led Ben to create an idea about electricity that was different from the idea proposed by Dufay.

Franklin's Views

There is only one kind of electricity, an electrical "fluid."

Electrical fluid is not created or destroyed; it moves from object to object.

When an object has its natural amount of electrical fluid, it is not electrified.

When an object gains or loses some of its electrical fluid, the object becomes electrified.

An object with a shortage of electrical fluid and an object with extra electrical fluid will attract each other.

When two objects have extra fluid or when two objects have a shortage of fluid, the two objects repel one another, because neither can make a contribution to the other to even out the fluid.

When an object with extra electrical fluid is touched by an object with a shortage of electrical fluid, electrical fluid is exchanged and both objects could end up not being electrified (with their natural amounts of fluid).

When objects are rubbed together, electrical fluid moves from one object to the other and both become electrified (one has extra electrical fluid and one has a shortage).

There is a tendency for electrical fluid to even out so that all objects have their natural amounts.

GUIDE TO ACTIVITY 5

Two Kinds of Electricity or One? Ben Franklin's Answer!

◆What is happening?

Students electrify the flag with balloon electricity. They then rub the strip of Plexiglas with silk and move the *silk* toward the electrified flag to discover that the flag is repelled. The silk must therefore have the same kind of electricity as the flag (balloon electricity). The strip of Plexiglas has Plexiglas electricity and the silk used in rubbing the strip of Plexiglas acquires balloon electricity.

In general, the object rubbed acquires one kind of electricity and the material used in rubbing acquires a different kind of electricity. Ben Franklin observed this and must have wondered why rubbing was necessary to electrify objects and why the object and the material used in rubbing the object acquired different kinds of electricity. In addition, Ben thought that it was strange that an object could be given two different kinds of electricity and end up not being electrified. These observations and his desire to explain them led Ben to create some new ideas about electricity and how objects became electrified.

After the suggestions for further study, six students become objects that trade units of electrical fluid and simulate Ben's ideas about electricity.

◆Time management

One class period (40–60) minutes should be enough time to complete the activity and discuss the results. If the simulation is added, more than one class period may be required.

◆Preparation

The materials used in this activity are the same as those used in Activity 4. See Activity 4 for preparation of materials.

◆Suggestions for further study

In this activity students use a rubber balloon and a foil flag to discover that a strip of Plexiglas and the silk used to rub the strip of Plexiglas acquire different kinds of electricity. Challenge the students to use a similar technique to see if a rubber balloon and the flannel used to rub that balloon acquire different kinds of electricity.

◆ Simulation procedure

1. Choose six students to represent objects. The rest of the students can observe and later might be involved in additional rounds of the simulation.

2. Pass out a strip and its paper clips to each of the six students.

3. Explain to everyone that the paper clips are the units of the electrical fluid that Ben described. Also, point out that the spaces on each strip represent the "normal" amount of electrical fluid for the object. Students should see that the objects (students) have different numbers of paper clips and spaces. When an object has a paper clip in each space the object

Materials

• Six strips of paper or thin cardboard about 5 cm wide and with the following lengths: 10, 12, 14, 16, 18, and 20 cm. Draw a line across each strip every two centimeters and attach a paper clip to each space on the strip. (See diagram)

is in its normal state and is not electrified. None of the six objects should be electrified at the start.

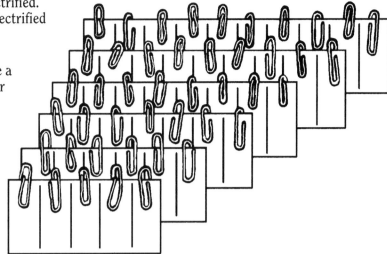

4. Choose one student and remove a couple of paper clips from his or her strip. Explain that this object has a shortage of electrical fluid (paper clips) and is now electrified. Add the paper clips taken from the first student to the strip of another student. The second student will now have more than the normal amount of electrical fluid and will be electrified. Both the object with a shortage of electrical fluid and the object with extra electrical fluid will be electrified. Return the extra paper clips to the first student's strip and point out that now both objects have the normal amount of electrical fluid and both objects are not electrified.

5. Pair the students up. The student pairs will represent objects that are rubbed together. There will be no rubbing; a hand shake will do. Each pair should decide which person (object) will give up electrical fluid to the other. The pair should also decide how many units of electrical fluid will be given up and acquired. At least two units of fluid—but not all—should be given up.

6. After the electrical fluid has been transferred, all objects will be electrified (half with shortages and half with extras). Because there is a tendency for objects to return to the normal state and not be electrified, the students (without talking) must circulate among themselves and make the necessary trades so that everyone ends up with the normal amount of electrical fluid. To add interest, students cannot trade with the person they initially traded with to become electrified. All paper clips must be on the strips and the strips must be in plain view all the time.

7. After the students make the trades and all objects return to normal, point out to the students that those objects (students) that had extras were attracted to those with shortages. Also point out that when two objects had extras they did very little, if any, trading. Likewise, for those objects with shortages not much, if any, trading took place—they avoided or repelled one another.
    Point out to the students that according to Ben there is only electrical fluid and that only electrical fluid moves from object to object. It is the extra or shortage that determines the "kind" of electricity that an object has. Also, make sure that the students see that the total number of paper clips remained the same during all the trading. Units of electrical fluid are not created or destroyed and are said to be conserved.

◆Answers

3. The flag with balloon electricity is <u>repelled by</u> the silk.

4. The flag with balloon electricity is <u>attracted to</u> the electrified Plexiglas.

5. Yes. The silk has balloon electricity.

6. No. The Plexiglas does not have balloon electricity.

7. No. The Plexiglas and the silk used to electrify the Plexiglas do not have the same kind of electricity.

8. Answer "c." When an object is electrified by being rubbed with a material, the object acquires one kind of electricity and the material acquires a different kind of electricity.

ACTIVITY 6 WORKSHEET

Ben's Electrical Sign Language (+ and –)

◆Background

Charles Dufay believed there were two kinds of electricity, which he described as "glass electricity" and "resin electricity." Ben Franklin, on the other hand, believed that there was only one kind of electricity or electrical fluid and that this fluid could move from one object to another. As an outgrowth of his beliefs, Franklin described electrified objects, not as having glass electricity or resin electricity, but as being positively charged (+), negatively charged (–), or neutral (no charge).

Franklin's way of identifying electrified objects is used today. In this activity, you will use Franklin's method to identify electrified objects as positively (+) or negatively (–) charged.

◆Objective

To understand what Ben Franklin meant when he identified objects as positively charged, negatively charged, and neutral or not charged
To use Franklin's way of describing electricity to determine charges on certain rubbed objects

◆Procedure

1. According to Ben Franklin, an electrified object with extra electrical "fluid" was called positively charged (+) and an object with a shortage of fluid was called negatively charged (–). The word "charge," as Ben used it, means to fill up or put one thing into another thing. A glass can be *charged* with water, a paintbrush can be *charged* with paint, and an object can be *charged* with electrical fluid. An overcharge of electrical fluid Ben called "positive" and an undercharge of electrical fluid Ben called "negative."

2a. Describe how the three glasses of water pictured below are like Ben's ideas about electricity. The line on the glass represents the "normal" amount of water in the glass.

_____

_____

Materials

For each group:
- a foil flag on nylon string
- a ruler or stick about 30 cm long
- a small, inflated balloon
- a strip of Plexiglas
- flannel cloth
- silk cloth
- a piece of glass (test tube, glass rod, drinking glass)
- a plastic tape cassette box
- a piece of nylon stocking
- a piece of plastic wrap
- a half sheet of overhead projection material rolled into a cylinder with a diameter of about 2 cm and taped at the ends and middle.
- other materials that can be electrified such as: plastic wrap on the roll, transparent tape on the roll, etc.

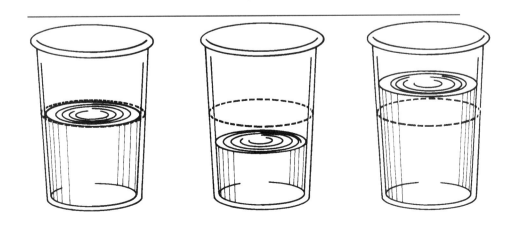

b.   Write a "+" on the glass of water that is like a positively charged object. Also, write a "–" on the glass of water which is like a negatively charged object.

3.   How would Ben figure out if a charged object had extra fluid (+) or a shortage of fluid (–)? He had no way of measuring electrical fluid so he resorted to guessing and was fully aware that his guess could be wrong. He guessed this way:

When glass was rubbed with silk, Ben guessed that the glass acquired extra electrical fluid (from the silk) and became positively (+) charged. The silk lost electrical fluid and became negatively (–) charged.

When resin was rubbed with wool, the resin lost electrical fluid and became negatively (–) charged. The wool acquired extra electrical fluid from the resin and became positively (+) charged.

We will not use glass or resin (from tree sap). Instead we will use balloons (rubbed with flannel) and strips of Plexiglas (rubbed with silk).

a.   Because an electrified balloon and an electrified piece of resin (– charged) repel one another, an electrified balloon must be (+ or –)_____ charged. Remember that two electrified balloons have the same kind of electricity and do in fact repel one another.

b.   Because an electrified strip of Plexiglas and an electrified piece of glass (+ charged) repel one another, an electrified strip of Plexiglas must be (+ or –)_____ charged.

c.   Summarize: The electrified balloon is_____ charged and the electrified strip of plexiglas is_____ charged.

4.   Determine Ben's charges on different electrified objects: Knowing that an electrified balloon is negatively (–) charged, how can we figure out the charges (+ or –) on other electrified objects? For example, how can we find out if a rubbed tape cassette case is + or – charged?

Step 1—Charge the foil flag: Instead of using a charged balloon directly, we will use the balloon to charge up the foil flag and use the flag to determine the charges of other electrified objects.

Hang the foil flag on its nylon thread from the ruler.

Give the flag a negative charge. To do this, use the same procedure you used in the last activity—Rub the balloon with flannel and touch the electrified balloon to the flag until the flag is repelled by the balloon.

a.   Because we have said the balloon is negatively (–) charged, the flag, which is repelled by the balloon, must be (positively or negatively) _____ charged. Once the flag is charged, move the balloon away from the flag.

b.   Step 2—Determine how electrified objects are charged: If an electrified object repels the – charged foil flag, the object must be (+ or –) _____ charged. If an electrified object attracts the – charged foil flag, the object might be (+ or –) _____ charged.

Using a – charged foil flag, determine how the following electrified objects are charged (+ or –). Before each test make sure that the flag is – charged. Before you test a new object, re-charge the flag with the electrified balloon (Step 1).

Object	Rubbed with	Attracts/Repels – foil flag	Charge
1. Plexiglas	silk	_____	_____
2. Tape cassette box	flannel	_____	_____
3. Glass	silk	_____	_____
4. Balloon	flannel	_____	_____
5. Piece of nylon stocking	plastic wrap	_____	_____
6. Roll of overhead projection material	flannel	_____	_____
7. _____	_____	_____	_____
8. _____	_____	_____	_____
9. _____	_____	_____	_____
10. _____	_____	_____	_____

GUIDE TO ACTIVITY 6

Ben's Electrical Sign Language (+ and –)

◆What is happening?

In this activity students review that Ben Franklin thought there was one kind of electricity and that an object was electrified if it had more or less than its normal amount of electrical fluid. Students learn of Ben's sign system for describing electrified objects. Objects with a normal amount of fluid were not electrified. Objects with extra electrical fluid were considered positively (+) charged. Objects with less than their normal amount were considered negatively (–) charged. The positive and negative signs mean respectively "more than normal" and "less than normal."

It is important to note that the word "charged" as used by Ben meant "to fill up or put one thing into another thing." A glass can be *charged* with water, a paintbrush can be *charged* with paint, and according to Ben, an object can be *charged* with electrical fluid. To be consistent with Ben's thinking and with the historical development of electrical concepts presented here, you would not wish to imply that something in or on the object was the charge because, according to Ben, the charge resulted from an object having an excess or a deficiency of electrical fluid. Electrical fluid was not the charge nor was it charged. Likewise, you would not wish to imply, at this point, that there are particles in objects which are positively or negatively charged and that these particles determine the charge of an object. According to Ben, "charge" simply meant that there was an excess or a deficiency of electrical fluid in an object.

Ben could not measure the amount of electrical fluid in an object so he had to resort to guessing which electrified objects had more or less electrical fluid. He knew he could be wrong. He guessed that electrified glass was positively charged (had extra electrical fluid) and that electrified resin was negatively charged (had a shortage of electrical fluid). Once he had made his guess he could then determine the charges of other electrified objects.

We still keep Ben's sign system today. However, Ben was wrong in that objects that are positively charged do not have an excess of something but actually have a shortage of something (negative charges or electrons) and that objects which are negatively charged do not have a shortage of something but an excess of something (negative charges or electrons). We will explore and explain Ben's mistake in future lessons.

Students should know that scientists sometimes make guesses, but that guesses are put to the test whenever possible. Only after learning more about the nature of matter and its electrical characteristics were we able to check Ben's guess. Ben never learned whether his guess was right or wrong.

◆Time management

This is a rather long activity. Although it might be finished in one class period of 40–60 minutes, it could be broken into two periods.

◆Preparation

Many of the materials used in this activity were used in previous activities. Some additional materials must be acquired. See the list of materials at the beginning of the activity. Roll half sheets of overhead projection material into cylinders and tape the cylinders at both ends and the middle. Encourage students to test electrified materials of their choice, using the blank slots in the data table to record their discoveries.

In the last activity, students used an electrified balloon to negatively charge the foil flag. Although students should be familiar with the charging procedure, it is tricky to get the foil flag to fly away and *stay away* from the charged balloon. You might save time by demonstrating how to negatively charge the flag. Point out that the charged side of the balloon (the rubbed side) should be moved toward the foil. Also, point out that it might be necessary to repeatedly charge the balloon and touch it to the flag until the flag flies away and stays away.

◆Suggestions for further study

Ben Franklin showed that when two objects are rubbed together both objects are electrified. He also showed that these objects have different kinds of electricity. Have students use a negatively charged foil flag to see if the flannel used in charging a balloon is positively or negatively charged.

Have students bring in other objects to determine the charge on them. When a piece of cellophane tape is pulled off a roll, is it positively or negatively charged? Charge a piece of writing paper by placing it on a desk top and rubbing it with the length of a pencil. Use the negatively charged flag to determine the charge on the paper. Sometimes paper coming out of a photocopy machine is charged. Check the charge on charged photocopy paper.

◆Answers

2a. The glass is like an object. The water is like Ben's electrical fluid. The glass with the water up to the line is like Ben's object which has a normal amount of electrical fluid and is not electrified. The glass with water below the line is like Ben's object which has less than the normal amount of electrical fluid. The glass with the water above the line is like Ben's electrified object which has more than the normal amount of electrical fluid.

b.   The glass with water above the line should be marked with a "+." The glass with water below the line should be marked with a "–."

3a. The electrified balloon must be <u>negatively (–)</u> charged.

b.   The electrified Plexiglas must be <u>positively (+)</u> charged.

c.   The electrified balloon is <u>negatively</u> charged and the electrified Plexiglas is <u>positively</u> charged.

4a. Because the balloon is negatively charged, the flag which is repelled by the balloon must be <u>negatively</u> charged.

b.   If an electrified object repels the negatively charged foil flag, the object must be <u>negatively</u> charged. If an electrified object attracts the negatively charged foil flag, the object might be <u>positively</u> charged. We must say, in the last sentence, that the electrified object *might* be positively charged, because at this point we have not developed conclusive evidence that different kinds of electricity attract. Because a foil flag which is not electrified would be attracted to any electrified object, the attraction might not be because of the kind of electricity on the flag.

Object	Rubbed with	Attracts/Repels – foil flag	Charge
1. Plexiglas	silk	attracts	+
2. Tape cassette box	flannel	repels	−
3. Glass	silk	attracts	+
4. Balloon	flannel	repels	−
5. Piece of nylon stocking	plastic wrap	attracts	+
6. Roll of overhead projection material	flannel	attracts	+
7. _____	_____	_____	_____
8. _____	_____	_____	_____
9. _____	_____	_____	_____
10._____	_____	_____	_____

ACTIVITY 7 WORKSHEET

Seesaws and the Modern View of Static Electricity

◆Background

We have been following the history of the ideas about static electricity. So far we have described ideas of Charles Dufay and Ben Franklin. The question becomes: What ideas of both men are correct and fit the modern view of static electricity? In order to answer this question, we have to explore, as we do in this activity, the modern ideas of static electricity. In the next activity we will compare this modern theory with the ideas of Dufay and Franklin to find out who was right.

◆Objective

To learn the modern ideas about static electricity

◆Procedure

1. Consider a seesaw made out of a ruler and a pencil (see below). The pencil is at the center of the ruler so the ruler will more or less balance. If you place three Life Savers™ on the left end of the ruler and three Life Savers on the right end of the ruler, the ruler will balance. So in one sense, 3 Life Savers + 3 Life Savers = 0 or a balanced seesaw. We have six Life Savers but three balance out the other three.

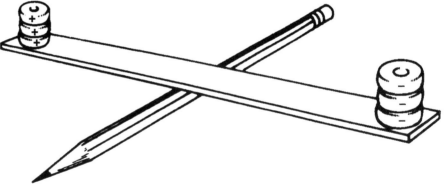

Suppose we mark Life Savers so that some are marked with a "+" sign and others are marked with a "–" sign. Furthermore, we'll stack only + Life Savers on the left end of the seesaw and only – Life Savers on the right end of the seesaw. The seesaw shows three +'s on the left balanced by three –'s on the right.

2a. **Challenge #1:** Start with a balanced seesaw—three +'s on the left balanced by three –'s on the right. Without adding or subtracting any + Life Savers on the left, what would you do with an extra – Life Saver to get the seesaw to tip down on the right (the negative side)? Make a drawing of the Life Savers on the tilted seesaw below.

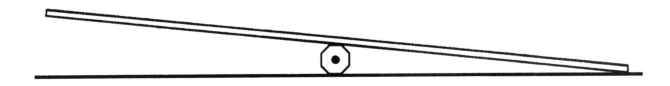

b. **Challenge #2:** Start with a balanced seesaw—three +'s on the left balanced by three –'s on the right. Without adding or subtracting any + Life Savers on the left, what would you do to get the seesaw to tip down on the left (the + side)? Make a drawing of the Life Savers on the tilted seesaw below.

In meeting the last two challenges, you have shown that you can get the seesaw to balance, to tip down on the left, and to tip down on the right by only adding or subtracting the – Life Savers. When the seesaw is tipped down on the left there are more + Life Savers than – Life Savers. When the seesaw is tipped down on the right there are more – Life Savers than + Life Savers. When the seesaw is balanced the number of + Life Savers equals the number of – Life Savers.

3. Now we will see how the seesaw example is like the modern view of static electricity. There are two different kinds of charges. Objects possess both positively and negatively charged particles. If you could microminiaturize yourself and take a trip in a tiny space ship into your chair, you would find that it consists of particles, called atoms, spread out in empty space. (You are sitting on mostly empty space!)

Atoms, you would discover, consist of smaller particles called neutrons, protons, and electrons. You would find that electrons are negatively charged, protons are positively charged, and neutrons have no charge. If you hung around the electrons and protons for a long time, you would discover that they never lose their charge and never have to be rubbed to acquire a charge. Electrons are always negatively charged and protons are always positively charged. In addition, you would find that there is the same amount of charge on each of these particles. You would not find one electron or proton more electrified than another.

If you journeyed throughout your chair and took a census, you would find that the number of electrons equals the number of protons. If you journeyed into other objects, you would make the same discoveries. All material objects have charged particles (electrons and protons) in them, even when those objects are not electrified. Just as the seesaw had both + and – Life Savers, all objects have both + and – particles in them. Just as the + and – signs were written on Life Savers, charges in real objects are on particles that make up those objects.

Two questions arise: If all objects have positively and negatively charged particles in them, why aren't objects always electrified? What happens with the charged particles in objects when the objects are electrified?

The charge on an object depends on the number of positive and negative charges in the object. The seesaw tipped down on the + side when there were more + Life Savers than – Life Savers. The seesaw tipped down on the – side when there were more – Life Savers than + Life Savers. The seesaw balanced when the number of + Life Savers was the same as the number of – Life Savers. In a similar manner, when an object has fewer negatively charged particles (electrons) than positively charged particles (protons), it has lost electrons, it is electrified, and it is said to be positively charged (more +'s than –'s). When an object has more electrons than protons, it has gained electrons, it is electrified, and it is said to be negatively charged (more –'s than +'s).

When the number of protons equals the number of electrons in an object, the object is said to be neutral or not charged. Even though the neutral object has positively and negatively charged particles in it, the electrical influence of the positively charged protons is balanced (or canceled out) by the electrical influence of the negatively charged electrons.

To Summarize:

Positively charged object: More positively charged particles (protons) than negatively charged particles (electrons).

Negatively charged object: More negatively charged particles (electrons) than positively charged particles (protons).

Neutral or uncharged object: The same number of positively charged particles (protons) and negatively charged particles (electrons).

In real, solid objects, the number of protons stays the same. The number of electrons changes to make the object positively or negatively charged.

a. When – charges are added to a neutral or uncharged object, that object becomes (negatively or positively) _____ charged.

b. When – charges are (subtracted from or added to) _____ a neutral or uncharged object, that object becomes positively charged.

Objects can have what is called a *net charge*. The net charge is the charge left over when the number of + and – charges are subtracted. For example, if an object has 5 + charges and 3 – charges, it has a net charge of + 2. If the same object has 5 + charges and 7 – charges, it has a net charge of – 2. If there are 5 + charges and 5 – charges, the object has a net charge of 0.

Example of the same object with different net charges

+ − + −	+ − + −	+ − + −
+ − +	+ − + −	+ − + −
+	+ − − −	+ −
Net = +2	**Net = −2**	**Net = 0**

c. Test your understanding by writing the net charge for each object pictured below. Remember, the net charge is the number of extra + or – charges in an object. A net charge of + 3 means that there are 3 more + charges than – charges.

A	**B**	**C**
+ − + −	+ − + −	+ − + −
+ − + −	+ − − −	+ − + −
+ +	− −	+ − + −
		+ −
A Net charge = _____	**B Net charge = _____**	**C Net charge = _____**

D	**E**	**F**
+ − + −	+ − + −	+ − + −
+ − + −	+ − + −	+ − + −
− −	+ − + −	+ −
	− −	
D Net charge = _____	**E Net charge = _____**	**F Net charge = _____**

d. Which of the previous two objects could be the same object but with different charges? _____ and _____. Hint: To get the seesaw (an object) to tip down on the negative side and then to tip down on the positive side, we added and subtracted only – Life Savers. Something remained the same when the – Life Savers were added and subtracted.

The net charges on objects determine whether electrified objects attract or repel and how much they attract or repel. When two objects have the same kind of net charge, they repel. When two objects have different or opposite kinds of net charges, they attract.

How strongly objects attract or repel is determined by how large the net charges are on the objects. The greater the net charges on the objects, the more strongly the objects attract or repel. Another factor that determines how much electrified objects attract or repel is the distance between them. The smaller the distance, the stronger the objects attract or repel. In other words, the closer the objects, the stronger the attraction or repulsion.

According to the modern view, how do objects acquire charges when they are rubbed together? In a previous activity, you discovered that when you rubbed two objects together, the objects received different charges.

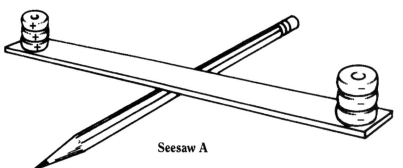

Seesaw A

Ben Franklin used this observation to argue that electrical fluid moved from one of the rubbed objects to the other. The electrical fluid lost by one object was gained by the other. Use your imaginary seesaws again to see how this might happen using the modern notions of static electricity.

Consider the two seesaws pictured, each with three + Life Savers and three – Life Savers, to

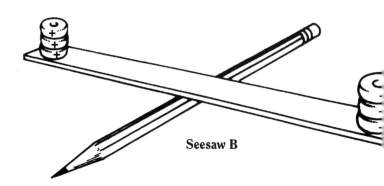

Seesaw B

be the two objects that will be "rubbed" together. What would you do to show what happens to produce two charged objects from rubbing? Remember that the number of positively charged particles (protons) in solid objects remains the same.

e.   Draw the Life Savers on the two seesaws below that represent two charged objects which have been rubbed together.

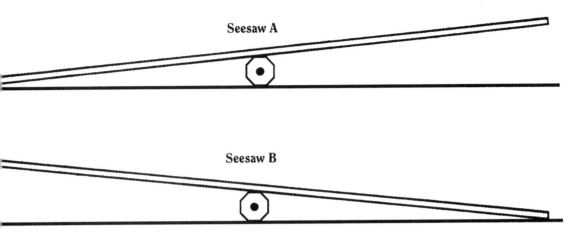

Seesaw A

Seesaw B

f.   When two objects are rubbed together, how do the resulting net charges of those objects compare? What is the net charge of seesaw A above? _____. What is the net charge of seesaw B above? _____.

Check: The number of – Life Savers lost by one object or seesaw should be the same as the number of – Life Savers gained by the other object or seesaw. There should be a net + charge on one object and the same net – charge on the other object. Charged particles (protons and electrons) are neither created nor destroyed. Negatively charged particles (electrons) move from one solid object to another. Positively charged particles (protons) stay put in solid objects.

Modern View

There are two kinds of charge: + and –.

These charges are on very small particles— protons (+) and electrons (–)—in objects.

Both protons and electrons are in objects, even when those objects are not electrified.

Electrons and protons do not acquire nor do they lose their charge. These particles have charge as one of their properties.

An object is neutral (not electrified) if the number of protons in it equals the number of electrons in it.

When two solid objects are rubbed together both become electrified as electrons move from one object to the other.

Protons in objects stay put.

Objects that gain electrons (–) become negatively charged and objects that lose electrons become positively charged.

The net charge on an object is the kind and number of charges left over when the number of – charges is subtracted from the number of + charges.

Different charges (+ and –) attract. The same kind of charges (both + or both –) repel.

Objects with large net charges attract or repel each other more than objects with small net charges.

The greater the distance between charged particles or objects, the less they attract or repel; the smaller the distance between charged particles or objects, the more they attract or repel.

GUIDE TO ACTIVITY 7

Seesaws and the Modern View of Static Electricity

◆What is happening?

This lesson is primarily a straightforward presentation of the modern view of static electricity. It may seem strange that the modern view is introduced so late in the module. Recall that through previous lessons we have been tracing the historical development of the ideas about static electricity. Prior to this lesson we have developed the ideas of Dufay and Franklin. Here we present the modern view. In the next lesson we will use the modern view developed in this lesson to answer the question: Who was right, Dufay or Franklin? The students will learn that both men were, in part, correct in their views. The purpose of this historical development is to help students understand that scientific ideas are invented in the minds of people, that scientists create different ideas about the same thing, and that new and better ideas replace the old ones.

The table on page 35 is the first comprehensive introduction of the modern views of electricity. Having the students memorize this information at this point in the text would probably not be helpful. By working through the remainder of the book, the students will come to learn these facts by repeated experimentation and discovery.

There may be concern at this point that students, in learning about "old, incorrect" ideas, may find those ideas acceptable and may, as a consequence, experience difficulty in giving them up to accept the modern view. Although students may experience some problem entertaining three different views, it should be pointed out that the main historical ideas were correct (Dufay—two kinds of charges; Franklin—only one kind of charge moves from object to object) and are part of the modern view. Therefore, there will be very few old ideas which the students will have to give up as they accept the new ideas. For the most part, the modern view of static electricity incorporates and integrates many of the old ideas. The observations students have made are correct and repeatable. In the modern view we retain Ben Franklin's language, so much of the language used to describe the observations is the same. The new view will simply better explain the observations students have made. In a future lesson, we will return to some of those observations and interpret them in light of the new view. These interpretations should help students better understand the modern view.

◆Time management

Two, perhaps three, class periods of about 40–60 minutes each should be enough time to complete the activity and discuss the results. If students are presented with the origins of modern static electricity (see "Suggestions for further study"), at least one additional class period will be needed.

◆Preparation

There are no materials for the students to manipulate in this activity. However, a demonstration of how the seesaw works might help students better understand the analogy and the related modern view of static electricity. A regular double pan balance might be used. The model of the seesaw shown in the activity is very sensitive and almost impossible to balance with both ends off the table.

◆Suggestions for further study

Where did this modern view of static electricity come from? Scientists sometimes make great strides in understanding by studying what goes on in the parts of things, and then using what they have learned to make sense out of how the whole thing works. For example, by studying how cells work, scientists might better understand how the living body works. In a similar fashion, by studying the smallest parts and pieces of matter, scientists might be able to figure out why materials are different, why changes occur, and why materials interact in different ways. It was by studying the smallest pieces of matter that scientists found out about what happens when objects become electrically charged.

The strategy of studying the smallest parts started in the 1890s when scientists focused their attention on studying the atoms that make up materials. Scientists eventually found that an atom consists of a nucleus and electrons which move in orbits around the nucleus. The nucleus, which is very small, contains most of the matter in an atom and consists of protons and neutrons. Scientists also discovered two kinds of charge (positive and negative). Positive charges are on the protons in the nucleus and negative charges are on the electrons. The electrons can be imagined to be zipping around the nucleus in unpredictable paths (see diagram at left). The neutrons in the nucleus have no electrical charge.

Atoms usually have the same number of electrons as protons and therefore have the same number of negative charges as positive charges. In other words, the net charge of atoms is zero and the atom is electrically neutral. If an object's atoms are electrically neutral, then the object itself is also electrically neutral. How then do objects become electrically charged?

Atom (not to scale)

The atoms of some materials hold tightly to electrons and the atoms of other materials hold loosely to electrons. When two different materials are rubbed together, the atoms of the materials get close together. When this happens, electron stealing goes on—some electrons move from atoms that hold loosely to electrons to atoms that hold tightly to electrons.

Atoms in flannel hold loosely to their electrons. Atoms of balloon material hold tightly to their electrons. When flannel is rubbed over a rubber balloon, the balloon atoms steal electrons from the flannel atoms. The result? Some balloon atoms have extra electrons and some flannel atoms have a shortage of electrons.

Electrons have negative charges, so rubbed balloon atoms have more negative charges than positive charges. The atoms are negatively charged, so the structure made from the atoms—the balloon—is negatively charged. Because flannel atoms lose electrons when they are rubbed against the balloon, the structure made from the flannel atoms—the piece of flannel—is positively charged.

In summary, the atoms in some materials hold loosely to their electrons. When these materials are rubbed they often give up electrons and become positively charged. Atoms in other materials hold tightly to their electrons. When these materials are rubbed they often gain electrons and become negatively charged.

Electrostatic Series

Holds most loosely
to electrons
(greatest tendency
to become + charged)

Holds most tightly
to electrons
(greatest tendency
to become – charged)

Glass
Wool
Cat fur/Human hair
Silk
Cotton
Wood
Cork
Rubber

Materials can be ordered according to how tightly their atoms hold on to electrons. The ordered list above is called an electrostatic series. Atoms in the materials toward the top of the list hold loosely to electrons. Atoms in the materials toward the bottom hold tightly to electrons. When any two of the materials are rubbed together, the one nearer the top of the list becomes positive and the other becomes negative. Although Plexiglas is not on the series, it must hold very loosely to its electrons because it easily becomes positively charged when rubbed with silk or cotton flannel.

It's important to point out some common misconceptions you may need to address at this point. There is the tendency to think that certain materials always become positively charged and other materials always become negatively charged. According to the above series, when cotton is rubbed with rubber, cotton becomes positively charged. When cotton is rubbed with glass, cotton becomes negatively charged. The charge acquired by cotton depends upon what the cotton is rubbed with. The static charges acquired by any two materials that are rubbed together depend on how tightly the atoms in those materials hold to their electrons.

Another misconception is that the rubbing of two materials results in electrons being "scraped off" one material and on to the other. Electrons are not scraped off one material like paint is scraped off a piece of wood. Also, friction has little to do with the charging. The rubbing merely allows the atoms of the two materials to get closer together so that electrons can be transferred.

◆Answers

2a. To get the seesaw to tip down on the negative side without touching the + side, the students should add – Life Savers to the negative side.

b.   To get the seesaw to tip down on the positive side without touching the + side, the students should subtract – Life Savers from the negative side.

3a. When – charges are added to a neutral or uncharged object, that object becomes <u>negatively</u> charged.

b.   When – charges are <u>subtracted from</u> a neutral or uncharged object, that object becomes positively charged.

c.   The net charges for the objects are:

A = +2; B = –4; C = 0;   D = –2; E = –2; F = 0

d.   The two objects that could be the same are the objects with the same number of + charges. Those objects are A and E because both have 6 positive charges.

e. The two seesaws showing charged objects resulting from rubbing should show that – Life Savers have been moved from the negative side of one seesaw and added to the negative side of the other seesaw. One seesaw should gain the one or two – Life Savers removed from the other seesaw.

f. The net + charge on one object should be equal to the net – charge on the other object.

ACTIVITY 8 WORKSHEET

Who Was Right, Dufay or Franklin?

◆Background

Dufay claimed that there were two kinds of electricity—glass electricity and resin (hardened tree sap) electricity. Franklin, on the other hand, claimed that there was only one kind of electricity and that this was a fluid. The amount of electrical fluid in an object determined whether that object was positively charged (extra fluid), negatively charged (shortage of fluid), or not charged at all (a normal amount of fluid).

Are there two kinds of electricity (Dufay) or is there one kind that moves around (Franklin)? The answer to this question will be determined by the modern ideas regarding static electricity.

◆Objective

To learn how the modern view of electricity compares with the views of Dufay and Franklin

◆Procedure

1.   Review the ideas of Dufay and Franklin.
Dufay believed:
• There were two kinds of electricity (glass and resin).
• Different kinds of electricity (glass and resin) attracted, and the same kinds (glass and glass or resin and resin) repelled.
Franklin believed:
• There was only one kind of electricity.
• This electricity (electrical fluid) could move from one object to another.
• Objects with more than their normal amount of electricity were positively charged (+ or extra), objects with less than their normal amount were negatively charged (– or shortage), and objects with their normal amount were not charged or were neutral.
• Positively charged objects (both with extra electrical fluid) repelled one another. Negatively charged objects (both with shortages of electrical fluid) repelled one another. Positively charged and negatively charged objects each had what the other needed and were attracted to one another.

2.   So . . . Who was right, Dufay or Franklin? Read each modern view statement and circle "agree," "disagree," or "no opinion" for Dufay and Franklin. An "agree" for Franklin would mean that he would agree with the modern view and a "no opinion" would mean that he would not have an opinion on this part of the modern view.

a.   There are two different kinds of electricity.

    Dufay would: agree   disagree   no opinion

    Franklin would: agree   disagree   no opinion

b.   When two solid objects are rubbed together and become electrified, only one kind of thing moves from one object to the other.

    Dufay would: agree   disagree   no opinion

    Franklin would: agree   disagree   no opinion

c.   Electrified objects that repel one another are electrically alike.

    Dufay would: agree   disagree   no opinion

    Franklin would: agree   disagree   no opinion

d. When a non-electrified, solid object becomes positively charged, something has been taken away from it.

    Dufay would: agree   disagree   no opinion

    Franklin would: agree   disagree   no opinion

e. When a non-electrified, solid object becomes negatively charged, something has been added to it.

    Dufay would: agree   disagree   no opinion

    Franklin would: agree   disagree   no opinion

3. Dufay was correct—there are two different kinds of electricity. Franklin was correct—there is only one kind of electricity that moves from object to object. Both men provided ideas that helped to further understanding of electricity. The modern view, however, shows both men's views to be incomplete and sometimes incorrect.

We may tend to think of our modern view as "true and absolutely correct." Ben's ideas were "modern" at one time and surely many believed them to be true and absolutely correct. Just as Ben's ideas gave way to better ideas, our modern view may at some time be found to be incomplete, incorrect, and even silly. In science, the door always remains open to new experiences and new ways of thinking about those experiences.

4. How did Ben get it backwards? In Activity 6, "Ben's Electrical Sign Language," you learned that Ben could not see electrical fluid and therefore had to guess which object gave up electrical fluid and which object gained electrical fluid when the objects were rubbed together. Ben guessed that when resin was rubbed with wool, the resin lost electrical fluid and the wool gained electrical fluid. The resin would have a negative charge because it would have a shortage of fluid and the wool would have a positive charge because it would have extra fluid.

The modern view keeps Ben's sign language. We still say that the resin is negatively charged and that the wool is positively charged. However, according to the modern view, the negative charges move from object to object. Therefore, the resin does not give up electrical fluid, as Ben guessed, it acquires negative charges from the wool. What Ben guessed was a shortage is actually an excess of negative charges.

a. You try it. Ben guessed that when the wool became positively charged the wool (gained or lost)

_____ electrical fluid. According to the modern view, the wool (gained or lost)

_____ negative charges. The wool is positively charged because it has (more or less)

_____ positive charges than negative charges.

Ben knew he was guessing. He never learned that his guess was wrong.

Franklin

One Kind of Electrical Fluid

+ Charge (Extra Fluid)

No Charge (Normal Amount of Fluid)

– Charge (Shortage of Fluid)

Dufay

Two Different Kinds of Electricity

Resin Electricity

Glass Electricity

GUIDE TO ACTIVITY 8

Who Was Right, Dufay or Franklin?

◆What is happening?

In this lesson students compare the ideas of Dufay and Franklin with some of the modern ideas about static electricity. They find that both Dufay and Franklin were, at least in part, right. Students should be helped to understand that scientific ideas are invented in the minds of people, that scientists create different ideas about the same thing, and that new and "better" ideas replace or modify the old ones. The ideas we think are true today may be replaced by the better ideas of tomorrow.

◆Time management

One class period (40–60) minutes should be enough time to complete the activity and discuss the results.

◆Preparation

None

◆Suggestions for further study

Challenge #1—When a balloon is rubbed with a flannel cloth, the balloon becomes electrified and acquires a negative charge.

Ben Franklin would say that the negative charge on the balloon means that . . .

The modern view would say that the negative charge on the balloon means that . . .

Challenge #2—When a balloon is rubbed with a flannel cloth, the cloth becomes electrified and acquires a positive charge.

Ben Franklin would say that the positive charge on the cloth means that . . .

The modern view would say that the positive charge on the cloth means that . . .

Challenge #3—The modern view of static electricity uses the idea of charge in two different ways. For example, we say that the balloon is negatively *charged* because it has more negative *charges* than positive *charges*. The balloon is *charged* because of its *charges*. Explain the difference between *charged* and *charges*.

◆Answers

2. So . . . Who was right, Dufay or Franklin?

a. Dufay: agree   Franklin: disagree

b. Dufay: no opinion or disagree   Franklin: agree

c. Dufay: agree (same kind of electricity)   Franklin: agree (same kind of charge)

d. Dufay: no opinion or disagree   Franklin: disagree

e. Dufay: no opinion or disagree   Franklin: disagree

4a. You try it. Ben thought that when the wool became positively charged, the wool <u>gained</u> electrical fluid. According to the modern view, the wool <u>lost</u> negative charges. The wool is positively charged because it has <u>more</u> positive charges than negative charges.

◆Answers to Suggestions for further study

Challenge #1—Ben Franklin would say that the negative charge on the balloon means that the balloon has lost electrical fluid and has less electrical fluid than it normally has.

The modern view would say that the negative charge on the balloon means that the balloon has received negative charges and has more negative than positive charges.

Challenge #2—Ben Franklin would say that the positive charge on the cloth means that the cloth has gained electrical fluid and has more electrical fluid than it normally has.

The modern view would say that the positive charge on the cloth means that the cloth has lost negative charges and has more positive than negative charges.

Challenge #3—The modern view of static electricity uses the term *charge* or *charged* in two different ways. Objects contain particles which carry positive electrical charges and other particles which carry negative electrical charges. So *charge* refers to the electrical property of certain particles in objects. An object is said to be *charged* when it has more of one kind of charged particle than it has of the other kind of charged particle. The *charged* object is electrified and shows electrical properties.

ACTIVITY 9 WORKSHEET

Expanding the View—Standing Still but on the Move

Materials

For each group:

• a foil strip (1 cm x 10 cm) bent and hung on the end loop of a nylon string as shown below. The strip is made by folding a 2 cm x 10 cm strip lengthwise. Fold over a corner of the strip to make one end pointed.

• a ruler or stick about 30 cm long

• a strip of Plexiglas

• flannel cloth

◆Background

The word "static" in static electricity means stationary, staying put, not moving. When a balloon is rubbed in one small place with a flannel cloth, the balloon is charged only where it has been rubbed. The extra negative charges in that rubbed area do not spread out over the entire surface of the balloon. They stay put, at least for a time. But charges are not always static. For example, to charge the spot on the balloon, extra negative charges had to be moved to that spot from the flannel cloth used in rubbing.

In this activity, we will use the modern view of static electricity to think about how charges move not only from object to object but, for some materials, within the object. We will look at something that stands still, but sometimes moves about.

◆Objectives

To learn about how charges move from object to object
To understand how the movement of charges determines whether objects are positively or negatively charged
To see how charges move within some objects

◆Procedure

1. To charge the foil strip: Hang the foil strip and its nylon thread from the ruler as shown below. Make sure the "arms" of the strip stick out horizontally. Gently touch the strip to remove any charge which might be on it.

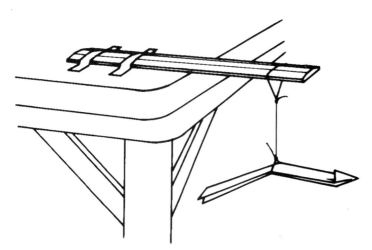

Now rub the strip of Plexiglas with flannel and touch the charged Plexiglas to the pointed end of the strip. The foil strip will likely jump away from the charged strip of Plexiglas. If it does not, gently move the Plexiglas away from the strip. Then move the Plexiglas back toward the foil strip to see if the foil strip is repelled. If the foil strip is not repelled by the electrified Plexiglas, repeat the procedure until the foil strip is repelled by the Plexiglas. You will discover later why only the point of the foil strip is touched.

2. Now we will trace the movement of charges that took place to charge the strip. First, let's review some modern ideas:

• When two objects are rubbed together and become electrified (charged), electrons with their negative charges move off one object and onto the other. The object that loses electrons becomes positively charged and the object that gains electrons becomes negatively charged.

• A negatively charged object has more negative charges than positive charges (more electrons than protons). A positively charged object has more positive charges than negative charges (more protons than electrons).

• A neutral object becomes negatively charged by receiving electrons. A neutral object becomes positively charged by losing electrons.

The picture at right shows the strip of Plexiglas and the flannel cloth before the rubbing. The strip of Plexiglas and cloth are neutral. Each have the same number of + and – charges.

These drawings show only a few charges. In reality, the number of neutral atoms in real objects is unbelievably large compared to the number of charges pictured.

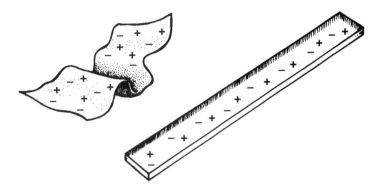

Before rubbing—charges on strip of Plexiglas and cloth

a.   Draw a picture of the charges on the strip of Plexiglas and cloth after the strip of Plexiglas has been rubbed by the cloth. A rubbed strip of Plexiglas is positively charged. Solid objects do not give up all of their electrons; so make sure that each object still has some negative charges after the charging.

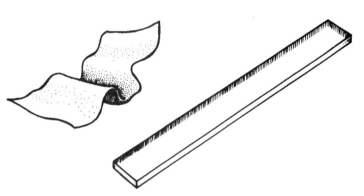

After rubbing—draw charges on strip of Plexiglas and cloth

b.   On the above drawing, draw an arrow from one object to the other showing which way the negative charges (electrons) moved.

c.   At the start the foil strip is uncharged or neutral. After touching the strip of Plexiglas, the foil strip flies away from (is repelled by) the positively charged Plexiglas. On the picture of the foil strip shown below, draw positive and negative charges to show how the strip is charged.

d.   Negative charges moved when the foil strip got its charge. The foil strip (lost or gained) _____ negative charges.

e.   When the foil strip lost or gained negative charges, where did those negative charges go?

_____

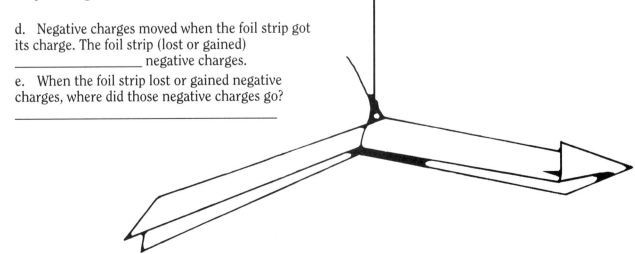

f. If you touch a charged foil strip with your finger, the strip loses its charge and becomes neutral. When the foil strip is touched, negative charges move from _____ to _____.

3. Touch the foil strip to make sure the strip starts out uncharged or neutral. Next, charge the strip of Plexiglas with the flannel. Touch only the pointed end of the foil strip with the Plexiglas. The pointed end of the strip should become charged and move away from the strip of Plexiglas. If the foil strip does not move away, repeat the procedure until the foil is repelled by the charged strip of Plexiglas. Touch only the pointed end of the strip with the strip of Plexiglas.

a. The Plexiglas touched only the pointed end of the foil strip. The Plexiglas has a positive charge on it, and it repels the pointed end of the foil strip. The pointed end of the strip must be (positively or negatively) _____ charged.

b. Use the charged strip of Plexiglas to test the charge on the "squared" end of the foil strip. What did you find out?

_____

_____

_____

_____

4. Which of the following statements best describes how charges moved to give a charge to the squared end of the strip? Remember the charged strip of Plexiglas only touched the pointed end of the foil strip.

a. Negative charges in the squared end of the foil were attracted to the positive charges in the strip of Plexiglas and moved along the foil to the pointed end of the foil and onto the strip of Plexiglas. The squared end of the foil became positively charged because it then had fewer negative charges than positive charges.

b. Positive charges moved from the strip of Plexiglas into the pointed end of the strip. Some of the positive charges moved down the strip to the squared end. The squared end then became positively charged because it had more positive charges than negative charges.

One of the above statements is true. Both however talk about charges moving from one end of the foil strip to the other end. Electrical charges can move around in some materials, called electrical conductors. Metals, such as the aluminum foil used in this activity, are good conductors of electrical charges.

Plexiglas does not allow charges to easily move around on it, but charges can be placed on Plexiglas. The same is true for the rubber in balloons. Materials which do not allow charges to move from one place to another in them are called nonconductors. Many non-metals are nonconductors of electrical charges.

GUIDE TO ACTIVITY 9

Expanding the View—Standing Still but on the Move

◆What is happening?

Students will use charged Plexiglas to positively charge a strip of aluminum foil hanging from a nylon thread. They will describe their observations in terms of the modern view of static electricity. In doing so, students should come to a better understanding of that view. Specifically, students will describe how negative charges move from object to object and how negative charges move within some materials (conductors) and not within others (nonconductors).

A rubbed strip of Plexiglas becomes positively charged because it loses negative charges (electrons) to the flannel. The foil strip, which is electrified by the strip of Plexiglas, becomes positively charged because it gives up negative charges to the positively charged Plexiglas.

In this activity, the positively charged strip of Plexiglas touches only the pointed end of the foil strip and yet the foil strip becomes positively charged at the squared end. Students should understand that for the squared end of the strip (untouched) to become positively charged, some negative charges had to be removed from that end. Those negative charges must have moved in the metal toward the pointed end of the foil. At the pointed end of the foil some electrons were transferred from the foil strip to the positively charged Plexiglas. In addition to electrons moving from the foil to the Plexiglas, the electrons must have moved on the foil. Those materials that allow electrons to easily move over and through them are called conductors. Metals are conductors. Conducting materials are contrasted with nonconducting materials such as Plexiglas and rubber. Although charges can be placed on nonconductors, charges do not easily move about on them.

◆Time management

One class period (40–60) minutes should be enough time to complete the activity and discuss the results.

◆Preparation

None

◆Suggestions for further study

Students could likely use more practice in applying the modern view of static electricity to observations they have made in previous activities. In this activity, a positively charged strip of Plexiglas was used to positively charge a foil strip. In previous activities, students negatively charged balloons by rubbing them with flannel. These negatively charged balloons were then used to give foil flags the same negative charge (charged flags were repelled by charged balloons). Have students repeat this charging of the flag with a charged balloon. Then ask the following set of questions:

1. When a rubber balloon is rubbed with a flannel cloth, the balloon becomes negatively charged.
• How did negative charges move when the balloon was electrified with the flannel cloth?
• How would you use the phrases "more negative charges than positive

charges" and "more positive charges than negative charges" to describe the charges on the negatively charged balloon and on the positively charged piece of flannel?

2. When a charged balloon is brought near a suspended foil flag, the flag at first is attracted to the balloon and then flies away, repelled by the balloon.
• When the flag is repelled by the balloon, what is the charge on the flag?
• How did negative charges move when the flag became charged?

3. When a charged flag is touched by a finger, the flag becomes uncharged or neutral.
• How did negative charges move when the flag was touched by a finger?

◆Answers

2a. The students' drawings should show more + than – charges on the strip of Plexiglas and more – than + charges on the cloth. The number of + charges on both objects should be the same as shown. Because positively charged objects tend not to give up all of their negative charges, there should be few negative charges left on the strip of Plexiglas.

b.   The arrow showing the movement of electrons should point from the strip of Plexiglas to the cloth.

c.   The foil strip should be positively charged because it was repelled by the positively charged strip of Plexiglas. The students' drawings of the foil strip, therefore, should show more + than – charges.

d.   When the foil strip became positively charged, it <u>lost</u> negative charges.

e.   When the foil strip <u>lost</u> negative charges, those negative charges moved *to the strip of Plexiglas*.

f.   When the foil strip is touched it loses its charge and becomes neutral. Negative charges move from <u>your finger</u> to <u>the strip</u>.

3a. The pointed end of the foil strip must be <u>positively charged</u> because it is repelled by the positively charged strip of Plexiglas.

b.   Because the squared end of the foil strip is also repelled by the positively charged strip of Plexiglas, the squared end must also be positively charged.

4.   The motion of the charges is best described by "a." The negative charges in the squared end of the foil strip were attracted to the positively charged strip of Plexiglas and moved down the foil to the pointed end and onto the strip of Plexiglas.

ACTIVITY 10 WORKSHEET

A Charge Detective: The Pie Pan Electroscope

◆Background

We have used the charged foil flag as a detector of other electric charges. Another way of detecting charges is with an electroscope. Although it is useful to know about how to use electroscopes to detect charges, it is more useful to expand our knowledge of electricity by figuring out how the electroscope works.

   In this activity, the primary focus will be on using some of the ideas presented in previous activities to imagine the movement and placement of charges in the electroscope. Then, from that imagined movement and placement, we'll figure out how the electroscope works.

◆Objective

To build an electroscope that detects charges on objects
To explain how the electroscope works by describing the movement and placement of charges in the electroscope when charged objects are brought near the pie pan

◆Procedure

1.   To make the charge detector or pie pan electroscope:

   Open up the paper clip and use an end to make two holes near the center of the pie pan. The holes should be about as far apart as the width of a paper clip.

   Use the end of the paper clip to put a hole very near one end of each of the two small (1 cm X 4 cm) foil strips. These holes should be large enough so that when the strips are placed on the paper clip, the strips hang freely side by side.

   Unfold the paper clip so it looks like an "S." Then open the wider end of the paper clip and thread it through one of the holes in the pie pan. Bend the end of the paper clip back into its original shape and guide the end back through the other hole in the pie pan. See the diagrams.

   Place the foil strips on the paper clip as shown. Carefully smooth out the strips so they lie close to one another and can move freely.

   Place the pie pan with its paper clip and foil strips over a clear glass container.

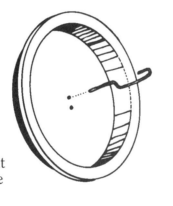

Materials

For each group:

To make a pie pan electroscope—

• one 11-cm-diameter disposable, aluminum foil pie pan. A 20-cm-diameter pie pan can also be used. The larger pie pan often collects a greater charge, but it is easily knocked off the glass.

• one regular size, metal paper clip

• two 1 cm x 4 cm pieces of regular weight (not heavy duty) aluminum foil

• one clear glass container (drinking glass, jar, beaker)

The glass container should be about 8 cm in diameter and at least 12 cm tall.

Other items: (Some of the same materials used in Activity 5)

• a small, inflated balloon

• a strip of Plexiglas

• flannel cloth

• silk cloth

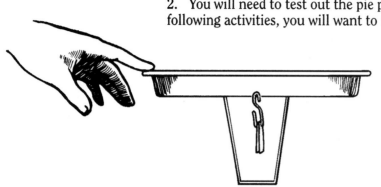

2. You will need to test out the pie pan charge detector. In some of the following activities, you will want to remove the charge from the electroscope before going ahead. To remove the charge or, in other words, to discharge the electroscope, gently touch the pie pan with your finger.

a. What happens to the foil strips of the electroscope when you hold a negatively charged balloon over the pie pan?

_____

b. What happens to the foil strips when the charged balloon is taken away from the pie pan?

_____

c. Predict what will happen to the foil strips when a positively charged strip of Plexiglas is held over the pan

_____

d. What actually happens to the foil strips when a charged strip of Plexiglas is held over the pan?

_____

e. When the foil strips are apart, are the kinds of charges on the strips the same or different?

_____

3. **Challenge:** What is the net charge of the foil strips when the charged balloon is held near the pie pan? When you held the negatively charged balloon over the electroscope, the foil strips moved apart. Because we know that like charges repel, the charge on the strips must have been the same to move the strips apart. The question to be considered now is: Were the strips positively or negatively charged?

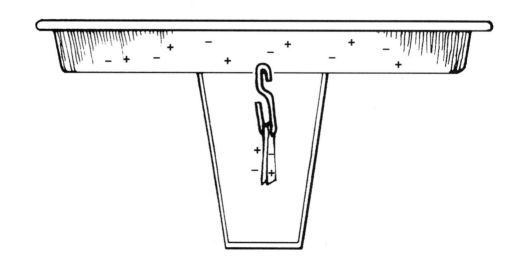

Knowing that the balloon was negatively charged and considering the following two ideas, we will answer the question.

Idea #1: Only negative charges (electrons) move in solid conductors (such as aluminum foil and metal paper clips). Positive charges (in the nuclei of atoms) are evenly distributed in solids and stay put.

Idea #2: The same kind of charges repel one another. Excess negative charges in conductors, therefore, tend to move as far as possible from each other.

The drawing at the bottom of page 50 shows what the charges look like in an electroscope that has no charge on it or which is not near a charged object. The number of positive charges and the number of negative charges are equal (represented by eight of each—positive and negative—in our drawing) and the charges are evenly distributed around the electroscope.

For this activity, the drawings show only a few charges on each object. In reality, the number of neutral atoms in real objects is unbelievably large compared to the number of charges pictured.

The following drawing shows only the positive charges in the electroscope. A "snapping or cracking" sound may occur as the balloon nears the electroscope. This means that electrons have "jumped" from one object to the other. If there were no such sounds and the balloon did not touch the pan, no charges should have been added to or taken from the electroscope. Because the electroscope starts out as neutral (no net charge), the number of positive and negative charges on the electroscope should be equal, even with the charged balloon held near the pan.

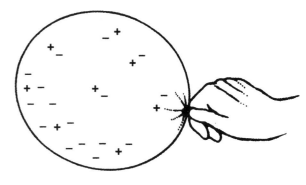

a. Considering the ideas above and knowing that the balloon is negatively charged, draw in eight negative charges on the electroscope shown in the diagram.

b. The net charge on each of the foil strips is (positive, negative, or zero (neutral))

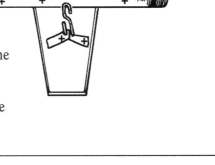

_____when a charged balloon is brought near the pan of the electroscope.

c. Why are the foil strips of the electroscope spread apart when the balloon is held near the pan?

_____

_____

d. Describe the movement of negative charges (electrons) on the electroscope when the balloon was brought near the pan.

_____

_____

e. The net charge on the entire electroscope is (positive, negative, or zero (neutral)) _____ when the charged balloon is held near the pan of the electroscope.

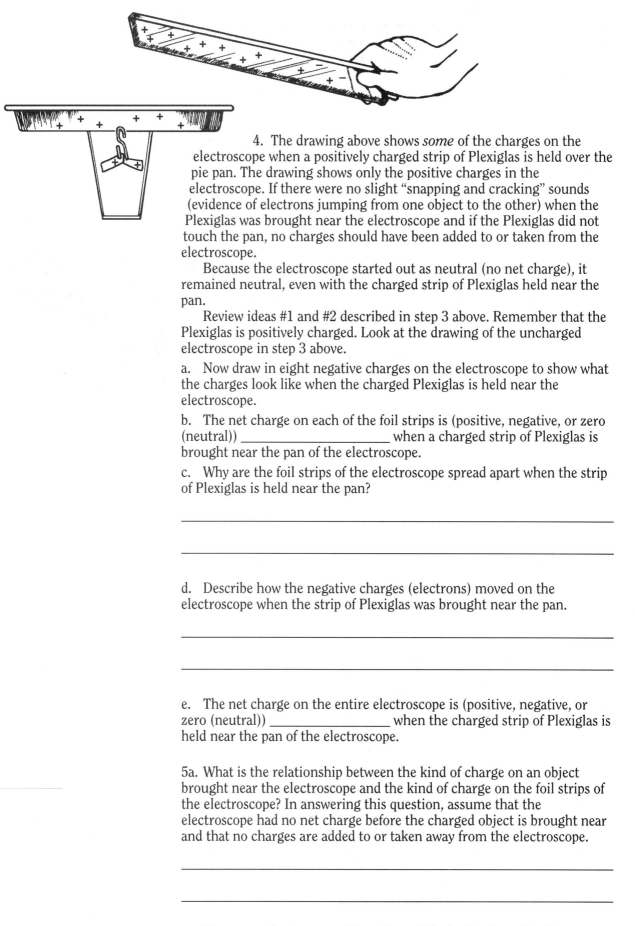

4. The drawing above shows *some* of the charges on the electroscope when a positively charged strip of Plexiglas is held over the pie pan. The drawing shows only the positive charges in the electroscope. If there were no slight "snapping and cracking" sounds (evidence of electrons jumping from one object to the other) when the Plexiglas was brought near the electroscope and if the Plexiglas did not touch the pan, no charges should have been added to or taken from the electroscope.

Because the electroscope started out as neutral (no net charge), it remained neutral, even with the charged strip of Plexiglas held near the pan.

Review ideas #1 and #2 described in step 3 above. Remember that the Plexiglas is positively charged. Look at the drawing of the uncharged electroscope in step 3 above.

a.   Now draw in eight negative charges on the electroscope to show what the charges look like when the charged Plexiglas is held near the electroscope.

b.   The net charge on each of the foil strips is (positive, negative, or zero (neutral)) _____ when a charged strip of Plexiglas is brought near the pan of the electroscope.

c.   Why are the foil strips of the electroscope spread apart when the strip of Plexiglas is held near the pan?

_____

_____

d.   Describe how the negative charges (electrons) moved on the electroscope when the strip of Plexiglas was brought near the pan.

_____

_____

e.   The net charge on the entire electroscope is (positive, negative, or zero (neutral)) _____ when the charged strip of Plexiglas is held near the pan of the electroscope.

5a. What is the relationship between the kind of charge on an object brought near the electroscope and the kind of charge on the foil strips of the electroscope? In answering this question, assume that the electroscope had no net charge before the charged object is brought near and that no charges are added to or taken away from the electroscope.

_____

_____

Keep your electroscope. You will use it in further investigations.

GUIDE TO ACTIVITY 10

A Charge Detective: The Pie Pan Electroscope

◆What is happening?

In this activity, students construct a homemade electroscope. They bring charged objects near the pie pan and observe that the foil strips move apart. The strips must have the same type of charge on them (both + or both –) because like charges repel one another.

When the negatively charged balloon is brought near the pan, the electrons (negative charges) on the pan are repelled by the negative charges on the balloon. Some electrons move from the pan down onto the foil strips. With more negative than positive charges on the strips, the net charge on each strip is negative. Because like charges repel, the negatively charged strips repel one another.

In a similar fashion, when a positively charged strip of Plexiglas is brought near the pan, the electrons on the pan and the strips are attracted to the positive charges on the strip of Plexiglas. Some electrons on the foil strips move from the strips onto the pan. This results in more positive charges than negative charges on the strips. The strips each have a net positive charge. Because like charges repel, the positively charged strips repel one another.

In both cases when the strips are apart, the net charge on the electroscope as a whole object is still zero, provided that no charges have been added to or taken from the electroscope. With a charged object near the electroscope, the charges within the electroscope are simply re-distributed and a localized net charge develops on the pan and on the foil strips, which move apart.

◆Time management

One class period (40–60) minutes should be enough time to complete the activity and discuss the results.

◆Preparation

To save class time and to facilitate the construction and use of the electroscope, you might want to cut out the 1 cm x 4 cm foil strips and put the holes near the very top of each strip. Make extra strips because a few will be damaged. Also, make up a few electroscopes and place them around the room so students can observe these models as they construct their own electroscopes. Note: The students will use these electroscopes again, so be sure to save them after this activity.

◆Suggestions for further study

How would an electroscope work if you replaced the metal paper clip with a plastic paper clip? Try it.

Remove the pie pan from the electroscope and hang the bent paper clip from some object (pencil, plastic pen, piece of index card, etc.) laid across the opening of the glass. Test out these different objects to see if they help or hinder the detection of charges.

Redesign the foil strips, or the entire electroscope, so the new design makes it easier to detect and see the effects of electrical charges. The electroscope used in this activity is not very portable and can be used only if held in an upright position. Can you design a portable electroscope which can be used when held in different positions?

◆Answers

2a. When the charged balloon is brought near the pan, the foil strips of the electroscope spread apart.

b.   When the charged balloon is taken away from the pan, the foil strips of the electroscope move back together. (This will occur only if the electroscope has not been touched or if no spark has jumped between the balloon and electroscope.)

c.   When a positively charged strip of Plexiglas is brought near the pan, the foil strips should also spread apart.

d.   When a positively charged strip of Plexiglas is brought near the pan, the foil strips spread apart.

e.   Charges of the same kind repel one another. Therefore, when the strips are spread apart, the kind of charges on each strip are the same.

3a. There should be 8 negative charges drawn on the electroscope. Most of the –'s should be on the foil strips. For example, there might be 4 –'s on each strip. The number of –'s on each strip should be the same or nearly the same. The net charge on each foil strip should be negative (more –'s than +'s).

b.   The net charge on each strip should be <u>negative</u>. The net charges could be equal (e.g., –2 and –2).

c.   Each strip has a net negative charge. Because like charges repel, the strips repel one another and move apart.

d.   The net negative charges on the balloon repelled the negative charges (electrons) on the pan. These negative charges on the pan moved down onto the foil strips and created net negative charges there.

e.   Because it is presumed that the electroscope was initially uncharged and because no charges were added to or taken from the electroscope, the net charge on the entire electroscope should be zero, even though parts of the electroscope show net charges.

4a. There should be 8 negative signs drawn on the electroscope. Most of the –'s should be on the pan. The net charge on each foil strip should be positive (more +'s than –'s) because the –'s moved from the foil strips up to the pan.

b.   The net charge on each strip should be <u>positive</u>. The net charges could be equal (e.g. +1 and +1).

c.   Each strip has a net positive charge. Because like charges repel, the strips repel one another and move apart.

d.   The net positive charges on the strip of Plexiglas attracted negative charges (electrons) on the pan and on the foil strips. The negative charges on the foil strips moved up onto the pan leaving net positive charges on the foil strips.

e.   Because it is presumed that the electroscope was initially uncharged and because no charges were added to or taken from the electroscope, the net charge on the entire electroscope should be zero, even though parts of the electroscope show net charges.

5a. The kind of charge on the object brought near an electroscope and the kind of charge on the foil strips are the same.

ACTIVITY 11 WORKSHEET

A Magical Electrical Touch

◆Background

When a charged object is moved near an electroscope, the foil strips of the electroscope move apart. When the charged object is moved away, the foil strips fall back together. It is possible, however, to get the leaves to remain apart after the charged object has been moved away from the electroscope. When the strips are apart, there is a charge on the strips.

In this activity you will discover how to use a charged object and a "magic touch" to get a charge that stays on the strips—even when the charged object is moved away from the electroscope. More importantly, you will explain your observations by figuring out how charges influence each other and move in the objects. You will see how science solves the mystery in the magic.

◆Objective

To learn how to use a charged object and a "magic touch" to get a charge that stays on the strips of an electroscope, even when the charged object is moved away from the electroscope

To describe how charges influence each other and move to produce the observations—in other words, to demonstrate and explain how an electroscope gets a net charge by using the charge induction method

◆Procedure

1. The following steps show how to use a charged balloon to charge an electroscope. When the electroscope is charged, the foil strips will stay apart without the charged balloon nearby.

Step 1—Gently touch the pan of the electroscope with your finger. This should remove any charge on the electroscope.

Step 2—Negatively charge a balloon by rubbing the balloon with flannel.

Step 3—Slowly move the charged balloon toward the pan of the electroscope. Do not let the balloon touch the pan. Start over at Step 1 if you hear any "snapping and crackling" noises as the balloon is moved toward the pan.

a. What happens to the foil strips when the charged balloon is held over the pan?

_____

Step 4—While holding the charged balloon over the pan, gently touch the pan with your finger.

b. What happens to the foil strips when your finger touches the pan?

_____

c. How would you describe the net charge on the foil strips when the pan is being touched by your finger?

_____

_____

Materials

For each group:

• one electroscope—see the previous activity for the materials and method of construction

• a small, inflated balloon

• a strip of Plexiglas

• flannel cloth

• silk cloth

Step 5—First remove your finger from the pan. Then move the charged balloon away from the pan.

d. What happens to the foil strips when the balloon is moved away from the pan?

_____

e. Is there a net charge on the foil strips? _____. If you followed the steps carefully, you should see evidence that the electroscope is electrified (charged). The method used in Steps 1 through 5 to place a charge on the electroscope is called a charge induction method.

2. Now that you have charged your electroscope, try some investigations with it.

Start with a charged electroscope. A charged electroscope has its foil strips spread apart when no charged object is near the pan. If you do not have a charged electroscope, charge your electroscope by following Steps 1 through 5 above.

Start with a charged balloon some distance away from the pan. Slowly move the charged balloon toward the pan of the charged electroscope and watch what first happens to the foil strips.

a. What happens to the foil strips as a negatively charged balloon is moved toward the pan?

_____

Start with a charged electroscope (Steps 1–5). Slowly move a charged strip of Plexiglas toward the pan.

b. What happens to the foil strips as a positively charged strip of Plexiglas is moved toward the pan?

_____

A charged electroscope can be used to detect the kinds of charges (+ or –) on objects brought near it.

c. When you have a balloon-charged electroscope, the foil strips of the electroscope will come together when a (positively or negatively) _____ charged object is brought near the electroscope.

Without a charged object near the charged electroscope, touch the pan of the charged electroscope with your finger.

d. Time for your magic touch. What happens to the foil strips when you touch the pan with your finger?

_____

3. You need to keep track of charges in order to explain the magical touch. When the negatively charged balloon is held over the pan of the electroscope (Step 3), the negative charges on the balloon repel the negative charges in the pan. Those repelled negative charges in the pan move down into the foil strips. The strips move apart because they both have a net negative charge. We say that the balloon has *induced* a charge on the electroscope. The pan part of the electroscope is positively charged and the foil strips are negatively charged.

For this activity, the drawings show only a few charges on each object. In reality, the number of neutral atoms in real objects is unbelievably large compared to the number of charges pictured.

While the charged balloon is held over the pan and the pan is touched (Step 4), the foil strips come together.

a. On the drawing below, show the negative charges that would be on the foil strips that hang together.

Just before the pan is touched there are extra negative charges on the foil strips.

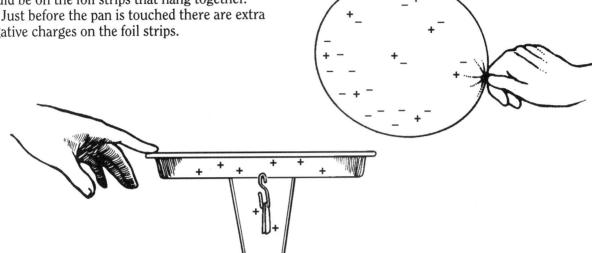

b. Where do the extra negative charges go when the pan is touched?

_____

_____

When first your finger and then the balloon are taken away (Step 5), the foil strips spread apart. This indicates that there is the same kind of net charge on each of the strips and that the electroscope is charged.

c. On the drawing below, show the negative charges as they might appear on the electroscope when its foil strips are apart.

d. The net charge on the foil strips is (positive, negative, or zero (neutral))_____.

e. The net charge on the electroscope is (positive, negative, or zero (neutral))_____.

f. The electroscope develops a (positive or negative)_____ charge when the pan of the electroscope is touched in the presence of a negatively charged object.

When an electroscope has been given a net charge through the use of a charged object and the magic touch, we say that the electroscope has been *charged by induction*.
Using this method, the charge
will remain on the electroscope
for awhile and does not depend
on having a charged object nearby

When a charged object is
brought near a previously neutral or uncharged
electroscope, the leaves move apart indicating that
they have the same net charge. It might be said that
there is a charge *induced* on the leaves by the charged
object. Note that the charge *induced* on the leaves by
the charged object remains only as long as the charged
object is near the electroscope. "Inducing a charge" and
"charging by induction" have slightly different meanings.

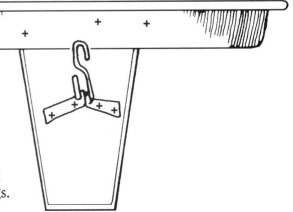

4. Keeping track of charges will help you explain two things: what happens when a charged object is brought near a charged electroscope, and what happens when you touch a charged electroscope.

Earlier, you moved a negatively charged balloon slowly toward a positively charged electroscope (charged by the balloon). As the charged balloon was brought near the charged electroscope, the foil strips of the electroscope moved together, indicating that there was no longer the same net charge on each of the strips.

a. Why do the foil strips come together as the negatively charged balloon is moved toward the pan of a positively charged electroscope? Hint: Electrons move within the electroscope as the negatively charged balloon is moved toward the electroscope.

_____

_____

_____

_____

When the charged balloon is not near the pan and the foil strips are apart, a touch of your finger will cause the foil strips to hang together again. When your finger is taken away, the foil strips continue to hang together and show no evidence of net charges.

b. What happens to electrons when your finger touches the pan and the foil strips come together again after being apart? Hint: Electrons move either from the finger and the electroscope or from the electroscope to the finger.

_____

_____

_____

_____

5. When the "magic touch" is used to place a charge on an electroscope, the electroscope gets a charge that is opposite to the charge on the object used in charging. A negatively charged balloon puts a positive charge on the electroscope. A positively charged strip of Plexiglas puts a negative charge on the electroscope.

When a charged object is brought near a charged electroscope, the charges on the two are opposite if the foil strips *first* move together. The charges on the two are the same if the foil strips *first* move further apart.

Save your electroscope. You will use it in the next activity.

GUIDE TO ACTIVITY 11

A Magical Electrical Touch

◆What is happening?

In this activity students learn how to charge an electroscope by using a charge induction method. They discover the method by using the standard procedure: hold a charged object close to the electroscope, momentarily touch the electroscope with your finger, and then remove the charged object. The students are also guided in formulating an explanation.

As in the previous activity, a charge will be induced on the electroscope (negatively charged balloon repels electrons down into the foil strips which spread apart). In the presence of the charged balloon, the pan of the electroscope will be positively charged and the foil strips will be negatively charged.

When the pan is touched the electrons congregated in the foil strips can get even further from the negative balloon by moving out of the electroscope and onto the finger. When first the finger and then the balloon are removed, the electroscope, having lost electrons to the finger, becomes positively charged. With net positive charges on the foil strips, the strips spread apart. Note that when a negatively charged balloon is used to induce the charge, the resulting net charge on the electroscope is positive.

Special Note: This activity offers the opportunity to discuss grounding. Electrons repel one another and tend to move as far as possible from each other. When the finger touches the pan and the student is electrically connected to the Earth (not insulated with rubber-soled shoes), electrons can flow to and from the Earth or ground through the student and his or her finger. The touch provides a pathway to the Earth so the electrons can get as far as possible from the concentrated source of electrons around the electroscope. The Earth also has an "unlimited" supply of electrons so when there is a concentration of positive charge in and around the electroscope, the electrons move from the Earth through the student's finger and into the electroscope.

◆Time management

Two class periods of 40–60 minutes each should be enough time to complete the activity and discuss the results.

◆Preparation

Check to make sure the electroscopes are in working order.

◆Suggestions for further study

Use a positively charged strip of Plexiglas in place of the charged balloon, and follow Steps 1–5 to induce a negative charge on an electroscope. Figure out at Steps 3–5 how electrons are moving on the electroscope. In Step 3 electrons are attracted by the Plexiglas up onto the pan and away from the foil strips. The strips momentarily acquire a net positive charge. In Step 4, electrons, attracted by the positively charged Plexiglas and the net positive charges on the foil strips, move from your finger onto the pan and down onto the foil strips. In Step 5 when the finger and then the Plexiglas are taken away, the foil strips and the electroscope are left with a net negative charge.

Use a charged electroscope to determine the kind of charge on a variety of rubbed objects. Record the kinds of charges (+ or –) on the various electrified objects. Remember, when an electroscope gets a net charge by the induction method, the charge on the electroscope is opposite that of the charge on the object used to induce the charge. Also, when a charged object is moved toward a charged electroscope, the foil strips *at first* move together if the charges are opposite; the strips *first* move further apart if the charges are the same.

Use the induction method to produce a net charge on an electroscope. Without touching the pan see how much time it takes for the foil strips to move back together. See if you can figure out how the humidity of the air influences how fast the strips move back together. How might you re-design the electroscope so that it keeps its charge for the longest period of time or for the shortest period of time?

Challenge: Get together with a group of students. Each group or team is to secretly use the magic touch method and either a charged balloon or charged strip of Plexiglas to place a charge on an electroscope. The challenge is for each team to figure out the charge on the other team's electroscope.

◆Answers

1a. The foil strips spread apart when the negatively charged balloon is held over the pan.

b. When your finger touches the pan, the foil strips come together.

c. There must be no net charge on the foil strips while they are hanging together.

d. When your finger and then the balloon are moved away from the pan, the foil strips spread apart.

e. Yes, there is a net charge on the foil strips.

2a. The foil strips of the charged electroscope move together as the charged balloon is slowly moved toward the pan.

b. The foil strips of the charged electroscope move further apart as the charged strip of Plexiglas is slowly moved toward the electroscope.

c. When you have a balloon charged electroscope, the foil strips of the electroscope will come together when a <u>negatively</u> charged object is brought near the electroscope.

d. When the pan of a charged electroscope is touched by your finger, the foil strips come together.

3a. The drawing should show few, if any, negative charges on the pan and a negative charge for each positive charge on the foil strips, because the foil strips are neither attracting nor repelling one another.

b. The touching must have something to do with why the strips come together. The extra negative charges that were on the strips must move out of the electroscope and into the finger as they get as far away as possible from the negative charges on the balloon.

c. The drawing might show two negative charges on the pan and one negative charge on each foil strip. The net charge on each strip would be positive and the net charge on the electroscope might be positive.

d. The net charge on the foil strips is <u>positive</u>.

e. The net charge on the electroscope is <u>positive</u>.

f. The electroscope develops a <u>positive</u> charge when the pan of the electroscope is touched in the presence of a negatively charged object.

4a. The foil strips of a positively charged electroscope have a net positive charge on them. When a negatively charged balloon is moved toward a positively charged electroscope, the foil strips move together and show that they no longer have a net positive charge. The foil strips become neutral because negative charges have been added to them. The negative charges move from the pan into the strips because they are repelled by the negatively charged balloon.

b.   When a positively charged electroscope (foil strips apart) is touched with a finger, the strips move together. Negative charges must move from the finger into the electroscope to neutralize all the positive charges.

ACTIVITY 12 WORKSHEET

Conducting a Charge: The Pie Pan Zapper

Materials

For each group:

• one electroscope (See Activity 10 for the materials and method of construction)

• one small, disposable aluminum pie pan (same type as used in the construction of the electroscope—11 cm or so in diameter)

• two rubber bands that fit across the small pie pan

• a strip of Plexiglas

• silk cloth

For the class:

• one large, disposable aluminum pie pan (20 cm or so in diameter)

• two large rubber bands stretched across the diameters of the pie pan to form an "X."

• one large piece of Plexiglas (about 20 cm square)

• silk cloth

• one fluorescent light bulb or tube (even one that is burned out)

• a couple of pieces of aluminum foil (about 20 cm X 30 cm each), a couple of pieces of notebook paper, a roll of cellophane tape, and a pair of scissors

• (optional) at least 2.5 m of insulated wire (remove about 3 cm of insulation from each end)

◆Background

You have been able to produce a net charge on an electroscope by using a charge induction method. In this activity you will produce a charge on the electroscope by using a direct (momentary) contact or conduction method. As a demonstration, you will see a charged pie pan light a fluorescent bulb. Then your task will be to figure out how to light the fluorescent bulb without touching the pie pan to the bulb.

In this activity you will make the connection between static electricity (electricity which stays put) and current electricity (electricity being conducted along or flowing within and between objects).

◆Objective

To see that static charges can be stored on an insulated conductor (pie pan) and then transferred to an object (fluorescent tube) either directly or along another conductor

◆Procedure

1. To make an Insulated Pie Pan (IPP): Stretch two rubber bands across the diameters of the pie pan to form a rubber band X in the middle of the pan. If you hold the bands at the X on the open side of the pan, you can avoid touching the metal pan. Because the rubber bands are electrical insulators and do not allow charges to move along them, you can touch the bands and still keep a charge on the pan.

2. You charged the electroscope using the charge induction method. Here you will charge the IPP using the same method.

Step 1—Touch the metal of the IPP to remove any charge from it.

Step 2—Rub a strip of Plexiglas with the silk cloth to place a positive charge on the Plexiglas.

Step 3—Place the IPP on the charged Plexiglas, making sure the metal part touches the Plexiglas.

Step 4—Briefly touch the metal of the IPP with your finger.

Step 5—Touching only the rubber band X (not the metal), move the IPP away from the charged Plexiglas.

There should now be a charge on the IPP. To see if there is a charge, try the following "nose test."

3. To see if there is a charge on the IPP, hold the IPP by the rubber band X and move the pan so it barely touches the end of your nose. If there is a charge on the pan and if the day is not too humid, you might feel a very tiny, painless "zap" at the end of your nose as a spark jumps from the pan to your nose. If a spark jumps, the pan will not likely have a net charge.

If you touch the metal part of the pan or if you wait too long, the IPP will lose its charge and will not zap your nose. You might have to try this a number of times, each time charging the IPP as described in steps 1–5.

When your nose or finger touches a charged IPP, the IPP loses its charge. We say that the IPP has been *grounded*. If you are not wearing rubber-soled shoes, you are likely to be electrically connected to the ground. This means that electrons can move through you to and from the ground. If there are extra electrons on the IPP, they repel each other. If you touch the negatively charged IPP, the electrons, repelled by one another, can move out of the IPP through you and spread out over the ground. If the IPP is positively charged and is touched, electrons move from the ground through you and into the IPP.

4. What happens to the charges in the IPP when the IPP is placed on a strip of positively charged Plexiglas before the IPP is touched by your finger? The positive charges on the Plexiglas attract the negatively charged electrons in the metal of the IPP. The electrons, which can move in metal, congregate toward the bottom of the IPP and close to the positively charged Plexiglas. This leaves more positive charges than negative charges in the top part of the IPP.

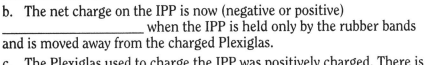

The electrons *do not* move from the metal pan onto the Plexiglas. This is because the Plexiglas is not a good conductor of electricity and does not allow electrons to easily move on it or into it.

a. When your finger briefly touches the metal part of the IPP, electrons flow (into the IPP from your finger or out of the IPP and onto your finger) _____.

b. The net charge on the IPP is now (negative or positive) _____ when the IPP is held only by the rubber bands and is moved away from the charged Plexiglas.

c. The Plexiglas used to charge the IPP was positively charged. There is the charge (on the IPP) and the charge (on the Plexiglas) doing the inducing. Those charges are (the same or different) _____.

5. You can transfer charge from the IPP to the electroscope by *conduction*. Use a charged strip of Plexiglas to induce a negative charge on an IPP. Touch the electroscope (not the IPP) to remove any charge from it. Then directly and briefly touch the metal part of the negatively charged IPP to the neutral electroscope.

a. After the charged IPP has touched the electroscope, the foil strips of the electroscope are (together or apart) _____.

b. Test the charge on the electroscope by moving a positively charged strip of Plexiglas slowly toward the charged electroscope. The foil strips of the electroscope move (together or farther apart) _____.

Recall that the Plexiglas is positively charged. Those positive charges should attract the negatively charged electrons in the charged electroscope and cause those electrons to move upward in the electroscope toward the Plexiglas.

c. If there were excess negative charges on the foil strips of the charged electroscope and those were drawn upward by the Plexiglas, then the foil strips should move (together or apart) _____.

d. Consider your answers above and determine the charge on the electroscope. The charge on the electroscope was (positive or negative) _____.

Recall that the electroscope got its charge when it was touched by the metal part of a *negatively* charged IPP.

e. The negatively charged IPP touched the electroscope and produced a (positive or negative) _____ charge on the electroscope.

When an object is charged by induction, it acquires the *opposite* charge of the object used to induce the charge.

f.   When the charged IPP touched and charged the electroscope, was the charge by induction? _____

The negatively charged IPP had an excess of electrons, all trying to get as far as possible from one another. When the charged IPP touched the electroscope there was metal to metal contact and the electrons could flow between the two objects.

g.   When the charged IPP touched the electroscope, which direction did the electrons flow? (from the IPP to the electroscope or from the electroscope to the IPP) _____.

When a charged object merely touches (does not rub) another object and gives a charge to it, we say that a charge is *conducted* (not induced). The charge is conducted from one object to another. This usually occurs when both objects are conductors of electricity. Electrons easily move in and on conductors of electricity. Insulators, which can have excess electrons, do not allow those electrons to easily move about.

In this case, both the IPP and the electroscope are metals and are good conductors. When the negatively charged IPP touched the electroscope, the excess electrons easily moved from the IPP into the electroscope and the electroscope became negatively charged. The foil strips of the electroscope separated because both had an excess negative charge.

6.   The electricity in your home is powerful and can be dangerous. The electricity we have been dealing with can hardly be detected by a sensitive nose. Is it possible then to use the charge on an insulated pie pan to get a blink of light from a fluorescent bulb like the ones used in homes and schools? You will see that it is by observing a demonstration.

The room will be darkened. The prong or prongs at one end of a fluorescent tube will touch a large metal object, such as a water pipe. The prongs at the other end of the fluorescent tube will be touched by a charged IPP (large size). You will not need sunglasses—the blink is quick. Watch carefully.

7.   **Challenge:** Can you blink a fluorescent tube from a distance? Assume you are given a pair of scissors, a piece of aluminum foil (about 20 cm X 30 cm), a piece of notebook paper, and some cellophane tape. Your challenge is to use these materials and a charged IPP to get a fluorescent tube to blink without allowing the charged IPP to get any closer to the tube than one and a half meters. A large piece of Plexiglas and a large insulated pie pan will also be used.

a.   Figure out a plan to solve the problem and describe or draw the plan below:

b.   Explain the solution by describing how electrons travel from the charged IPP to the tube.

_____

_____

_____

_____

Describe your solution and explanation to the rest of the class. See if your solution or one like it works.

GUIDE TO ACTIVITY 12

Conducting a Charge: The Pie Pan Zapper

◆What is happening?

The students have produced a net charge on an electroscope by using the charge induction method. In this activity they produce a charge on the electroscope by using a direct (momentary) contact or conduction method. An insulated pie pan (IPP) is charged by induction using a positively charged strip of Plexiglas. The negatively charged pie pan, held by the rubber bands, is touched to the end of a student's nose and a slight zap is experienced. The negatively charged IPP is also touched to a neutral electroscope and the electroscope becomes charged (foil strips move apart).

The charge on the electroscope is negative like that of the charged IPP. When the charged IPP and the neutral electroscope are touched together, extra electrons on the charged IPP move (are conducted) on to the electroscope which becomes negatively charged. The emphasis is on electrons moving in and between conducting materials (metals).

The students see a demonstration showing how a charged IPP can be used to get a fluorescent tube to blink. The emphasis here is on electrons moving (being conducted) from the IPP through the tube and causing the tube to briefly light or blink.

The students are then challenged to figure out how to use a piece of aluminum foil, notebook paper, cellophane tape, and a pair of scissors to get the tube to blink when the charged IPP can be no closer to the tube than one and a half meters. The students solve the problem by taping strips of aluminum foil together to make a strip. The strip is attached to one end of the tube and then is strung out over a distance of one and a half meters by the students holding the strip with loops of notebook paper that act as insulators. A charged IPP is touched to the end of the strip. The electrons move in the strip and the tube blinks.

The emphasis here is on electrons (negative charges) being conducted (moving) along a conductor. For a brief moment, an electrical current flows in the strip. A link is made between static electricity and current electricity.

◆Time management

Two class periods (40–60 minutes each) should be enough time to complete the activity and discuss the results. More time might be needed for students to solve the challenge. The challenge might be given as homework and then solution plans tried out during the next class period.

◆Preparation

Make sure that the electroscopes are in working order. See Activity 10 for directions on constructing pie pan electroscopes. Make sure the students hold the charged, insulated pie pan only by the rubber bands. If they touch the pan with their fingers, the pan will likely lose its charge. The rubber bands do not conduct electrical charges and therefore act as insulators. Answer 6 details how to perform the fluorescent tube demonstration.

Caution: Fluorescent tubes break easily, producing large, sharp ends. Additionally, the mercury vapor within tubes is poisonous. It might be safer to work with smaller tubes than larger ones.

◆Suggestions for further study

In this activity, a charged strip of Plexiglas has been used to induce a charge on the insulated pie pan (IPP). Can a negatively charged balloon be used to induce a charge on an IPP? Describe how electrons move when a balloon-charged IPP touches an electroscope. What charge is on the IPP and what charge does the electroscope end up with?

What is the longest wire (aluminum foil strip) that can be used to conduct a charge from the IPP to the fluorescent tube? If insulated bell wire is used as a conductor, what is the longest stretch of wire that can be used to conduct a charge from the IPP to the fluorescent tube?

Experiment to invent a "super zapper." Try different sizes of charged Plexiglas and insulated conductors (e.g., an aluminum cookie sheet) to see how much charge can be induced on an insulated conductor.

◆Answers

4a. When your finger briefly touches the metal part of the IPP, electrons flow <u>onto the IPP from your finger</u>.

b. Negative. The IPP received electrons from the finger.

c. Different. The charge induced on an object is different from the charge on the object used to induce the charge.

5a. After the charged IPP has touched the electroscope, the foil strips of the electroscope are <u>apart</u>.

b. The foil strips of the electroscope move <u>together</u> when a positively charged strip of Plexiglas is moved toward the electroscope.

c. The foil strips should move <u>together</u>.

d. The charge on the electroscope was <u>negative</u>.

e. The negatively charged IPP touched the electroscope and produced a <u>negative</u> charge on the electroscope.

f. No. The charge was not by induction.

g. When the charged IPP touched the electroscope, the electrons flowed <u>from the IPP to the electroscope</u>.

6. How to perform the demonstration: Place a fluorescent tube or bulb with the prong or prongs of one end touching a large metal object such as a water pipe. The prongs at the other end of the tube will be touched by the charged IPP. Darken the room and use a large piece of charged Plexiglas to induce a charge on a large insulated pie pan. Touch the charged IPP to the prong or prongs of the "free" end of the tube. The tube should briefly flash or blink.

Some questions and answers associated with the demonstration:

Do both prongs on each end of the tube have to touch the metal object or the charged IPP? No. Only one prong at each end needs to be touched.

Will the bulb light if it does not touch the large metal object or the pipe? No. In order for the bulb to light, electrons must pass through the bulb. When the prongs on the end of the fluorescent tube touch a pipe or large metal object, the extra electrons which are given the tube by the charged IPP are able to pass through the tube and the pipe and spread out over the ground. This is called grounding.

What makes the bulb blink or light up? When the atoms of some materials are "hit" by electrons, the electrons give some of their energy to the atom and we say the atom becomes "excited" with this extra energy. The atoms can also become excited with the extra energy they receive from light falling on them. Excited atoms do not stay excited for very long. They go back to being unexcited by giving off the extra energy. Sometimes the energy given off is in the form of light that we can see and sometimes the energy given off is invisible.

A fluorescent tube or bulb is filled with a small amount of mercury vapor. The inside of the glass tube is coated with a white, chalky material made up of phosphors. When electrons move through the mercury gas in the tube (as they do when the charged IPP touches the prongs), the electrons hit the mercury atoms and give them extra energy. The excited mercury atoms then give up this extra energy in the form of ultraviolet radiation. Ultraviolet radiation is "so violet" (ultra-violet) that our eyes cannot see it. This ultraviolet light hits the atoms in the phosphors and excites those atoms. The excited phosphor atoms then give up the extra energy in a form of white light that we can see.

7a. One solution to the problem is:
• Cut the aluminum foil into about eight strips (each about 2.5 cm X 30 cm).
• Tape the strips together to make an aluminum strip wire about 2.5 meters long. Tape both sides of the strips where the strips overlap. This will insure that the strips always touch one another.

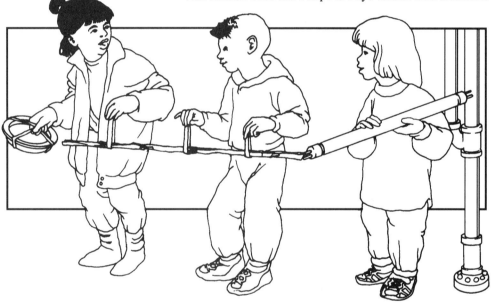

• Tape one end of the strip to the prong (or prongs) of the fluorescent tube. Make sure the other end of the tube touches a large metal object or a water pipe.
• Tear the notebook paper into strips and use the strips (loops) to hold the foil wire off the floor and to prevent the wire from touching anyone. If the wire is touching anyone when the IPP touches the wire, the charge will go into the person and not down the wire to the bulb.
• Induce a charge on a large IPP and touch the charged IPP to the free end of the wire (at least 1.5 m from the tube). The tube should give a faint and brief blink of light.

b.   When the charged IPP touches the wire, the extra electrons on the charged IPP move into the wire and along the wire (a conductor) to the prongs on the end of the tube. From the prongs, the electrons move through the mercury gas and into the prongs at the other end of the tube. From the prongs, the extra electrons move into and spread out over the large metal object.

Of prime importance here is that students see the movement of electrons down the aluminum "wire" as the flow of electricity or electrical current. This is similar to what will be occurring when students explore current electricity in future activities.

ACTIVITY 13 WORKSHEET

Back to the Beginning: Why Are Uncharged Objects Attracted to Charged Objects?

◆Background

The study of static electricity began when people long ago observed that a rubbed piece of amber (hardened tree sap) attracts bits of paper, hair, or plant material. In Activity 1 you observed that a rubbed balloon or strip of Plexiglas likewise attracts objects such as paper, hair, instant coffee, aluminum foil, pepper, and gelatin. These objects, which are not charged themselves, are attracted to charged objects.

We therefore, at first glance, cannot explain the attraction by saying that "objects with opposite charges attract" because the object attracted has no net charge and cannot be "oppositely charged." Why then are uncharged objects attracted to charged objects? This is the main question to be answered in this activity.

◆Objective

To explain why uncharged objects are attracted to charged objects

◆Procedure

There are slightly different answers to the question, "Why are uncharged objects attracted to charged objects?" The answers depend on the nature of the uncharged material. In this activity we will look at the attraction of metal (aluminum foil), paper, and water.

1. Conductors are materials in which electrons can easily move from one place to another. In solid conductors the nuclei of atoms (and the positive charges in them) vibrate back and forth and, for the most part, do not move from one location to another in the solid. Metals, including aluminum foil, are good conductors and allow electrons to freely move in or on them.

When a positively charged object such as a strip of Plexiglas is brought near a piece of aluminum foil (a good conductor), the negatively charged electrons are attracted to the positively charged strip of Plexiglas. Because the electrons are free to move in the foil, the electrons move to the side of the foil closest to the positively charged strip of Plexiglas. This results in the foil being negatively charged near the strip and being positively charged on the side away from the strip.

Look at the drawings of the foil flags and decide:

Materials

For each group:
- one Styrofoam cup
- one paper clip
- a cup of water
- a wide container to catch water
- a strip of Plexiglas
- silk cloth

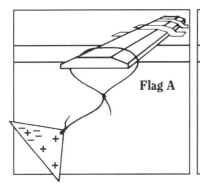

Flag A

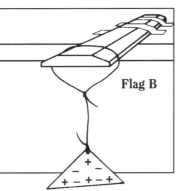

Flag B

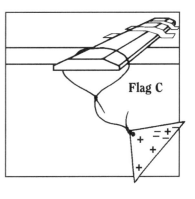

Flag C

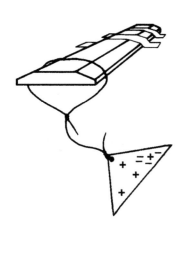

a.   Which flag (A, B, or C) shows the charges when no charged object is nearby? _____

Which flag shows the charges when a positively charged strip of Plexiglas is held to the left of the flag? _____

Which flag shows the charges when a positively charged strip of Plexiglas is held to the right of the flag? _____

The closer charges (or charged objects) are to one another the stronger they attract or repel. The farther away they are from one another the less they attract or repel.

Notice in the drawing at left that the negative charges in the foil flag are closer to the positively charged strip of Plexiglas than are the positive charges. The positive strip of Plexiglas is attracting the negative charges on the near side of the foil and is repelling the positive charges on the foil that are farther away. Notice also that the net charge on the flag is zero because the number of positive charges is equal to the number of negative charges. *Remember, these drawings show only a few charges. In reality, the number of neutral atoms in real objects is unbelievably large compared to the number of charges pictured.*

b.   Use the idea of distance and strength of interaction to explain why the foil flag is attracted to the strip of Plexiglas.

_____

_____

_____

_____

If a negatively charged balloon is brought near a neutral foil flag, the flag would be attracted to the balloon just as it is attracted to the positively charged strip of Plexiglas.

c.   Draw 4 –'s on the foil flag below to show the charges on the flag when the negatively charged balloon is near.

d.   Use the idea of distance and strength of interaction to explain why the foil flag is attracted to and moves toward the balloon.

_____

_____

_____

_____

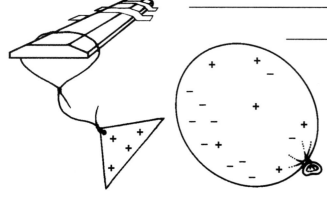

2.   Nonconductors are materials, such as paper, that have electrons that are held rather tightly to the atoms and are not free to move from place to place in the object. In the atoms of these materials the electrons orbit around the nuclei. If a charged object is brought near, the electrons in the atoms are pulled or pushed so they take a

more oblong path around the nuclei. When this occurs, the atom itself acquires a positive end and a negative end and is said to be electrically polarized.

When the atoms are polarized, the positive end of one atom is attracted to the negative end of a nearby atom. The polarized atoms then line up in a head to tail arrangement.

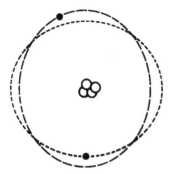

The drawing near the bottom of this page shows this head to tail arrangement of atoms in a piece of paper which is attracted to a negatively charged object.

Note how the atoms at the edge of the paper closest to the charged object are oriented: with their positive ends closest to the negatively charged object. One side of the paper is positively charged and the other side is negatively charged. One side of the paper is closer to the charged object than the other side.

a. Use the idea of distance and strength of interaction to explain why the piece of paper is attracted to the negatively charged object.

_____

_____

_____

_____

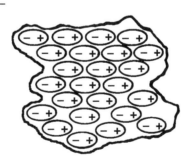

3. Can a stream of water be bent? How attractive is water? Use the end of a paper clip to punch a small hole in the bottom of a Styrofoam cup. While holding the cup over a catch container, fill the cup with water and adjust the size of the hole until a thin, smoothly flowing stream of water exits the bottom of the cup.

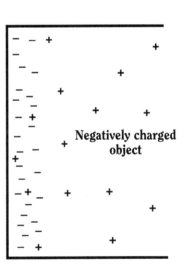

(Not to scale)

While one person holds the leaky cup with its stream of water flowing into the catch container, another person rubs a strip of Plexiglas with a piece of silk and moves the strip of Plexiglas toward the stream of water.

a. Describe what happens to the stream of water when a charged object (strip of Plexiglas) is brought near.

_____

_____

We have described how a charged object can distort the movement of electrons around the nucleus of atoms and make the atoms polarized. The molecules (groups of interacting atoms) in some materials are polarized

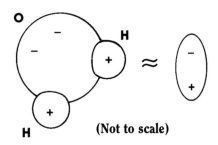

(Not to scale)

even when there is no charged object nearby. These polarized molecules have positive and negative ends to them. Water molecules are polarized.

There is a positive region around the hydrogen end of the water molecule and a negative region around the oxygen end of the water molecule. When a charged object is brought near water, the ends of the water molecules are attracted and repelled by the charged object. The molecules line up in a positive to negative, head to tail arrangement. The result is that one surface of the water stream is positively charged and the opposite surface is negatively charged.

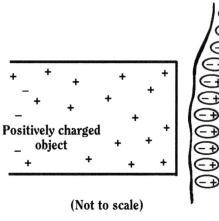

Positively charged object

(Not to scale)

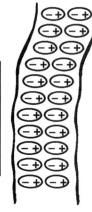

The drawing to the left shows the head to tail arrangement of water molecules as the stream passes by a positively charged object.

Note that the surface of the water closest to the charged object is covered with the negative ends of atoms. The surface of the stream farthest from the charged object is covered with the positive ends of atoms. One side of the stream is positively charged and the other side is negatively charged. One side of the stream is closer to the charged object than the other side.

b. Use the idea of distance and strength of interaction to explain why the stream of water is attracted to the strip of Plexiglas.

_____

_____

_____

_____

GUIDE TO ACTIVITY 13

Back to the Beginning: Why Are Uncharged Objects Attracted to Charged Objects?

◆What is happening?

In this activity the students learn how objects that have no net charge of their own can be attracted to charged objects. They learn that the charged object causes a reconfiguration of charges in the attracted object and that this reconfiguration results in the attracted object having a positive end or side and a negative end or side.

Because the side of the attracted object closest to the charged object is opposite in charge, the attraction is stronger than the repulsion of the far side of the object. Due to the differences in distance, attraction is stronger than repulsion and the object moves toward the charged object.

◆Time management

One class period (40–60 minutes) should be enough time to complete the activity and discuss the results.

◆Preparation

None

◆Suggestions for further study

Almost everyone has discovered that a rubbed balloon will stick to the wall. The balloon is negatively charged and the wall is uncharged and is usually a nonconductor. Use the ideas from this activity to explain why the balloon is held to the wall. Recall that when two objects interact, both exert forces on each other.

It is possible to electrostatically deflect a stream of water. Is it possible to electrostatically deflect a stream of dish washing detergent, baby oil, or other materials?

Rather than have teams of students "make a bend in the stream," you could demonstrate the electrostatic deflection of a stream of water. This could be turned into a problem for the students to solve: Without moving the leaky cup or the catch container and without touching the water, get the stream of water to hit the catch container at a different place. Teams of students would have to come up with solution plans which you would direct.

Using the ideas of electrostatic attraction described in this activity, invent a new gadget for making life easier or cleaner or healthier or more fun.

◆Answers

1a. Flag B shows its charges when no charged object is nearby.

Flag A shows its charges when a positively charged object is held to its left.

Flag C shows its charges when a positively charged object is held to its right.

b. The foil flag is attracted to the positively charged strip of Plexiglas because the electrons in the flag are attracted to the Plexiglas and consequently migrate to the side of the flag nearest the Plexiglas. However, the protons in the flag are repelled by the Plexiglas. So the flag is both pushed and pulled by the strip of Plexiglas. Because the negative side (attracted) is closer to the strip of Plexiglas than the positive side (repelled), the attraction is greater than the repulsion and the flag moves toward the charged strip of Plexiglas.

c.   The +'s and −'s on the flag should be equal in number and the positive charges should be evenly distributed over the flag. The negative charges in the flag are repelled by the negative charges in the balloon and should be drawn on the side of the flag away from the balloon.

d.   The foil flag is attracted to the negatively charged balloon for the following reasons. The flag's positive side is attracted to the negatively charged balloon and the flag's negative side is repelled by the negatively charged balloon. The flag is both pushed and pulled by the balloon. However, because the positive side (attracted) is closer to the balloon than the negative side (repelled), the attraction is greater than the repulsion and the flag moves toward the charged balloon.

2a. The explanation for why the piece of paper is attracted to the negatively charged object is the same as that for the flag, above. The only difference is that the electrons in the paper do not move from one place to another in the object; the atoms simply align in a head to tail arrangement to create positive and negative areas of the surface on the paper.

3a. When a charged strip of Plexiglas is brought near a stream of water, the water should be attracted to the strip of Plexiglas.

b.   The explanation for why the stream of water is attracted to the positively charged strip of Plexiglas is the same as that for the flag and paper above. The only difference is that molecules rather than atoms align in a head to tail arrangement to create a positive surface and a negative surface on the stream of water.

ACTIVITY 14 WORKSHEET

Zap, Cling, Sift, and Stick—Static Electricity in Our Lives

◆Background

Static electricity is very much a part of our daily lives. We will explore its role by explaining how that extra zap is added to a good night kiss, how lightning is created and how lightning rods protect buildings, how photocopy machines work, how smoke stack scrubbers use static electricity to "scrub" particles from the smoke, how the products that reduce that embarrassing static cling perform their magic, and how and why Van de Graaff generators can cause hair-raising experiences.

◆Objective

To describe how static electricity is a part of our everyday lives

◆Procedure

1. You might have shuffled across a rug and then experienced a little extra zap from a goodnight kiss or the light switch. In both cases, there was somewhat of a shock and emotion had little to do with its cause.

As you walked over the rug, your shoes interacted with the rug. You (and the rug) acquired an electrostatic charge. The rubbing either resulted in you acquiring extra electrons from the rug or you giving some of your electrons to the rug. When you gave your goodnight kiss, you either attracted electrons from the one you kissed or you gave up the extra electrons to the one you kissed.

In a similar fashion, you either acquired electrons from or gave electrons to the light switch. In any case, electrons jumped the small gap between you and the other person or light switch. During the jump, molecules in the air acquired energy and gave it back in the form of heat, light, and sound energy which you observed as a spark.

When two objects rub together, there is the possibility of achieving charges on both objects. When airplanes and cars move through the air and over the ground, charge can build up on them. If the object's tires are insulators and keep electrons from moving to or from the ground, significant and possibly dangerous charges can build up on vehicles.

For example, airplanes can acquire a rather large charge. This charge must be discharged after the plane lands and before anyone connected to the ground touches the outside of the plane. Airplanes are discharged by touching them with a conductor which is connected to the ground. If by chance the plane has not been discharged and you are the first person to leave, you might get an extra "push" off the plane as you become a conductor of charges between the plane and the ground—zap! These zaps or sparks are, however, carefully avoided, not only to maintain passenger and airline employee comfort, but also to avoid igniting any jet fuel which might be around the airplanes.

2. Although you may have already associated the tiny, household static electricity sparks with thunderous lightning bolts, the association has not always been obvious to people. In 1750 Ben Franklin sent a letter to the Royal Society in which he described an experiment to determine "whether clouds that contain lightning are electrified or not." Ben felt that the experiment had to be performed as close as possible to the clouds, so he

proposed that a man stand on an insulated stool in a box placed at the top of some high tower or steeple. An iron rod would extend upward from the man to some 6 or 8 meters and when a cloud passed overhead sparks would jump between the rod and the man (in Ben's terms "draw fire" from the man).

If that seemed too dangerous, and it was, Ben proposed an equally dangerous alternative in which the man in the box would use a piece of wax to hold a wire that extended from the ground up into the box. When a cloud passed overhead, the man was to move the wire toward the rod to see if sparks would jump between the wire and the rod. If there were sparks similar to those observed in the laboratory, then there would be some evidence that clouds were electrified.

At the time Ben proposed this experiment there were no high towers in Philadelphia, so Ben would have to wait. In the meantime, however, a French physicist, d'Alibard, tried out Ben's experiment with some minor modifications and confirmed the expected stream of sparks.

Before Ben had learned of d'Alibard's results, Ben himself solved the problem of getting the rod high in the sky by attaching the rod to a kite which was flown into a cloud. To the rod was tied a hemp string which descended to the ground. Both a key and a silk ribbon, which served as an insulator, were tied to the end of the string. Ben held on to the silk ribbon as he flew the kite into the storm. When he was about ready to give up, he noticed that the loose threads at the end of the string stood apart and appeared to avoid one another (like charges repel). Ben immediately moved the knuckle of his hand to the key and "drew fire" as an electrical spark jumped. The zap which Ben experienced confirmed his belief that clouds contain lightning and are electrical.

Ben continued his study of "cloud electricity" by erecting a rod on the chimney of his home. An insulated wire ran from the rod down through the house and attached to an iron water pump. Ben was then able to compare cloud electricity from the wire with the static electricity he could produce in his laboratory. He concluded from his comparisons that clouds were most often negatively charged and sometimes positively charged. We now know that whole clouds do not have a single charge but are oppositely charged on the top and bottom. Most clouds are negatively charged on the bottom and positively charged on the top.

When a cloud with a negatively charged base moves above the ground, the negative charges in the ground are repelled, leaving the surface of the ground positively charged. There is an electrical attraction between the bottom of the cloud and the ground beneath the cloud. When the charges become large enough, there is a great electrical discharge ("spark") in the form of a bolt of lightning. Thunder occurs as a result of the air rapidly heating up from the spark.

Ben sought not only to understand but to use his understanding to make life better for all. He was both a scientist and an engineer. From his observations and ideas regarding static electricity, Ben created and promoted the notion that any tall building could be protected from lightning strikes if a pointed rod was attached to the top of a building and the rod was connected with a thick wire to a metal stake driven into the ground. The notion was not readily accepted. There was much controversy as to whether the rod prevented a strike or attracted a strike and directed the electricity harmlessly to the ground. Even Ben wavered on this point. There was further controversy over whether the end of the rod should be pointed or round.

From what we know today, the lightning rod does not prevent a lightning strike by discharging a cloud; but it does safely conduct a lightning bolt to the ground when the bolt strikes. The shape of the end of the rod has little to do with the effectiveness of the rod.

3.   The photocopy machines in most offices and schools depend on static electricity for their operation. The black material that becomes the letters on the sheets of paper is a fine powdery material called toner which is electrostatically attracted to those areas that will become letters. The trick is, however, getting those very tiny letter areas charged without charging the rest of the area. The trick is performed with an amazing material called a photoconductor. Some good photoconductors are selenium, arsenic, tellurium, and their alloys. Photoconductors are insulators or nonconductors in the dark and conductors of electricity in the light. This means that while in the dark the photoconductor will hold on to any charge given it; but in the light, the charge on the photoconductor can be conducted away. In a photocopy machine a metal drum or plate has a thin coat of photoconducting material (usually selenium) on its surface.

• In the dark the plate (or drum) is given a positive charge.

• The light from the sheet that is being copied is projected on the plate (or drum). Where the light hits the plate, the photoconductor becomes a conductor and the positive charge leaks off to the metal part of the plate. Where the light does not hit the plate (where the letters are "projected") the photoconducting material remains a nonconductor, holds on to the positive charge, and does not conduct it to the metal part of the plate. What remains is a plate that has positive charges only where the letter areas are projected.

• That fine, powdery material called toner (plastic with carbon black in it) is given a negative charge and is brushed over the surface of the partially charged plate. The negatively charged toner is electrostatically attracted to the positively charged letter areas.

• Paper is then rolled over the plate and the toner sticks to the paper. Next the paper is run through hot rollers and the toner is melted into the paper to form permanent letters. The plate is cleaned and becomes ready for the next sheet.

This description of the workings of a photocopy machine does not begin to describe the technological ingenuity which has gone into developing photocopy machines. Engineers had to figure out how to design, make, and control toner (which is not simply carbon collected from a burning candle), how to charge the photoconductor plate and the toner, how to clean the plate and move and heat the paper, and how to do all of this rapidly and with ease.

4.   Hot gases and the particles in those gases are the by-products of many industrial processes. These gases and particles are vented into the air through smoke stacks. Electrostatic scrubbers are used to both reduce air pollution and to recycle some of the materials that go up in smoke. Scrubbers are based on the idea that oppositely charged objects attract. First the smoke passes through an area where the particles are given negative charges. The negatively charged particles are then attracted to objects within a positively charged duct, stick to them, and fall to the ground where they are collected for disposing or recycling. Some of the collected materials from smoke stacks are used to make toner for photocopy machines.

Caution: Do not try any of Franklin's investigations (or any investigations) having to do with the electricity of clouds and lightning. You will be risking your life. Franklin was extremely lucky . . . extremely lucky.

5. Whenever we have different kinds of materials rubbing one another, there is the possibility that those materials will acquire opposite static charges and will cling to one another. This occurs in clothes driers and sometimes with the clothes we wear. There are products on the market that reduce sticky laundry and that help us avoid what advertisers call "embarrassing static cling." These products are made with materials that contain molecules which are highly polarized. Polarized molecules have positively and negatively charged ends.

Some materials made for use in clothes driers are soaked in a solution that contains positively charged substances. The result is that there are positively charged locations which attract electrons. If electrons are attracted away from negatively charged objects and given over to positively charged objects, there is a reduction in attraction between the objects and static cling is reduced—embarrassment is gone and laundry can be more easily sorted!

Comb transfers charge (electrons) from belt to sphere

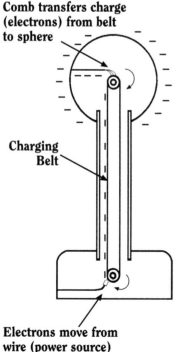

Charging Belt

Electrons move from wire (power source) onto belt

6. An interesting device occasionally found in laboratories and science museums is the Van de Graaff generator. The machine is used to create large electrical charges on the surface of a hollow sphere. In the classroom and museum the generator is used to perform static electricity demonstrations; including the one in which a student's hair stands out in all directions (hair raising). The student stands on an insulated stool and places his or her hands on the hollow sphere of the generator. The generator is turned on and a charge is produced on the sphere and on the student touching the sphere. The student's hair stands out because the strands of hair have the same charge on them and hence repel one another.

At the bottom of the generator a charge is placed on a belt made of an insulating material. The belt moves up inside the sphere and carries the charge with it. Inside the sphere and connected to the sphere is a metal comb which collects the charge from the belt. The charges repel one another and move as far as possible from one another to the outside surface of the sphere. The inside surface of the sphere is uncharged and therefore can receive more charges from the belt. As the process continues, a charge can be created on the surface of the sphere.

GUIDE TO ACTIVITY 14

Zap, Cling, Sift, and Stick—Static Electricity in Our Lives

◆What is happening?

This activity asks for little action from the students. Nevertheless, the activity should prove interesting to students because it deals with the role that static electricity plays in common objects and events.

◆Time management

One or two class periods (40–60 minutes each) should be enough time to complete the activity.

◆Preparation

This "activity" is presented in a direct instruction format. You may wish to use the information presented here to create a more inquiry-oriented form of instruction in which students are challenged to figure out the next step. For example, rather than state that a positive charge is induced in the ground under a cloud with a negatively charged base, challenge the students to describe what should happen to the electrons in the ground when a negatively charged cloud base is over the ground.

◆Suggestions for further study

Obviously, no students should be encouraged to replicate any of Ben Franklin's lightning experiments. Ben was lucky he was not electrocuted by a bolt of lightning. Students may want to do some library work on Ben Franklin and try to re-construct some of his more harmless electricity contraptions. Beware, however. One of Ben's static electricity generators produced a charge sufficient to kill a large turkey.

Lightning is a fascinating and complex subject. Interested students might want to read further about the different kinds of lightning and how charges are created in clouds.

Challenge students to make their own version of a Van de Graaff generator without using household electricity.

Under supervision and with the aid of a photocopy repair person, the students could explore the workings of an actual photocopy machine. How does the particular machine perform some of the functions described in the activity? How does the machine charge the plate or drum? How is the plate or drum cleaned after a copy is made? How does the machine sense that it is out of toner or paper?

MODULE 2

Current Electricity

◆Introduction

•How do light bulbs work?

•What is a short circuit?

•What is the difference between series and parallel circuits?

Answering these questions requires an understanding of the principles of current electricity—the effects of moving charges in wires and electrical devices.

The activities in Module 2 provide practice in designing circuits, analyzing the flow of electricity in circuits, and predicting circuit behavior.

◆Instructional Objectives

After completing the activities for Module 2, you should be able to

• state the conditions necessary for a bulb to light [Activities 15 and 16]

• explain the concept of open and closed circuits [Activity 17]

• construct a device to test whether a material is a conductor or nonconductor of electricity [Activity 18]

• identify the differences between series and parallel circuits [Activities 19, 20, and 21]

• define the following electrical terms: current, volts, resistance (ohms), and watts [Activities 22, 23, 24, and 25]

ACTIVITY 15 WORKSHEET

Lighting a Bulb With One Battery and One Wire

Materials

For each group:

• one #48 flashlight bulb

• one "D" battery (dry cell)

• one 20-centimeter piece of wire (#22 plastic-coated wire with plastic removed from the ends)

! The electricity used to run electrical devices in homes and schools can be dangerous! Do not experiment with or investigate this electricity. Do not take apart any device that runs on electricity coming from cords plugged into wall sockets.

◆Background

Many electrical cords in your home are made of two strands of wires. Many electrical plugs have two prongs. From these observations you may conclude electrical devices require at least two wires. But in this activity you will discover at least four different ways of lighting one bulb with one battery and only one wire.

◆Objective

To explore the conditions necessary for lighting a bulb with one wire and one battery

◆Procedure

1. **Challenge:** Discover four different ways of lighting the bulb with one wire and one battery. As you test different arrangements, draw pictures of arrangements that light the bulb and arrangements that do not light the bulb. Try to figure out what must happen to get the bulb to light with one battery and one wire. (Hint: The bulb and the battery each have two places which must be touched.)

You may wish to use the following pictures of a bulb, battery, and wire to draw your arrangements.

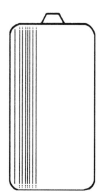
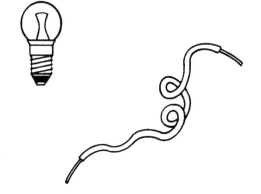

Arrangements which light

Arrangements which do not light

2. Write a postcard to send to a friend and describe hints that would help your friend quickly light the bulb in four different ways. Do not describe each of the four different ways. Do not use diagrams and use the fewest number of words you can. Try to provide only key ideas.

GUIDE TO ACTIVITY 15

Lighting a Bulb With One Battery and One Wire

◆What is happening?

In this activity students will discover four different ways of lighting a bulb with one battery and one wire. They will learn that the bulb has two parts (the bump on the bottom and the thread on the side) that must be touched (either directly or indirectly through the wire) to the opposite end of the battery. They will also discover that it doesn't matter which end of the battery directly touches either part of the bulb.

◆Time management

One class period (40–60 minutes) should be enough time to complete the activity and discuss the results.

◆Preparation

The wire will have to be cut to 20 cm lengths. If plastic-coated or enamel-coated wire is used, about 4 cm of plastic or enamel must be removed from each end of the wire so that 4 cm of bare wire shows at each end. Beware—there is an enamel-coated wire that is easily mistaken for bare copper wire. The enamel coating on this wire (like the plastic coating on other wires) is a nonconductor and must be scraped or sanded off the ends of the wire before the wire can be used as a conductor of electricity. Test the bulbs and batteries to make sure they are in working order.

◆Suggestions for further study

Challenge: Eliminate the wire and find other objects to use with the battery to get the bulb to light.

Can you get a bulb to light if the wire from the end of the battery only touches the dark material between the thread and the bump of the bulb?

Draw a tricky arrangement that looks like it should light the bulb but does not light the bulb.

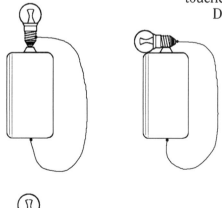

◆Answers

1. The diagram to the left shows the four different ways to light the bulb with one wire and one battery.

2. The bulb has two parts (the thread and the bump) that must be touched. The battery has two ends (bump end and flat end) that must be touched. One part of the bulb must touch (directly or indirectly through the wire) one end of the battery and the other part of the bulb must touch (either directly or indirectly through the wire) the other end of the battery. It does not matter which end of the battery directly touches a part of the bulb.

ACTIVITY 16 WORKSHEET

Predictions, Two-Wire Lighting, and Holding It All Together

◆Background

You have learned how to light a flashlight bulb with one wire and a battery. In this activity, you will put your knowledge to the test by predicting whether or not the bulbs in certain one-wire arrangements will light. You'll also test those predictions. Next you'll try some two-wire bulb lighting and examine a bulb holder (socket) and a battery holder.

◆Objective

To make and test predictions about bulb lighting in given arrangements, to create two-wire bulb lighting arrangements, and to determine the purpose of bulb sockets and battery holders

◆Procedure

1. Make some predictions: Without testing the arrangements first, circle the number on the batteries of those arrangements below that will light the bulb.

2. Now test your arrangements. Were your predictions right? Write the word "light" near the bulb of each arrangement that lights the bulb.

Materials

For each group:
• one #48 flashlight bulb
• one "D" battery (dry cell)
• two 20-centimeter pieces of wire (preferably #22 plastic-coated wire with plastic removed from ends)

For part 4:
• one battery holder (a thick rubber band and two attached Fahnestock clips)
• one bulb holder (socket)

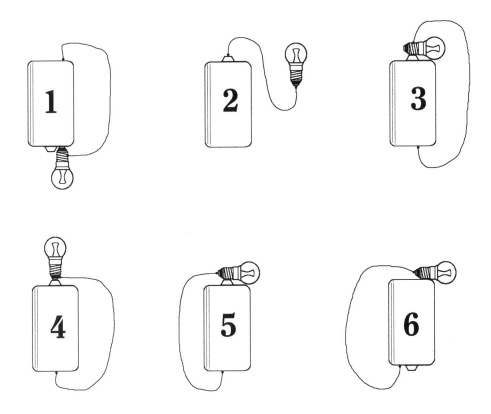

3. **Challenge:** Use two wires and one battery to discover different ways of lighting the bulb without the bulb directly touching the battery. Draw the arrangements below.

4. You probably found it difficult to hold the wires to the right places on the batteries and bulbs.

Challenge: Discover how to use the battery and bulb holders to get the bulb to light. The bulb holder (or socket) is nothing more than a contraption that holds the bulb and connects the wires to the thread and bump parts of the bulb. Also, the battery holder is nothing more than a contraption that securely connects the wires to the ends of the battery.

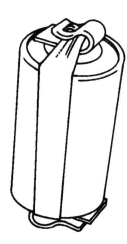

Bulb holders

Battery holder

GUIDE TO ACTIVITY 16

Predictions, Two-Wire Lighting, and Holding It All Together

◆What is happening?

The students have learned how to light a flashlight bulb with one wire and a battery. In this activity, students put their knowledge to the test by predicting whether or not the bulbs in certain one-wire arrangements will light. They test those predictions. Next, they invent two-wire bulb lighting arrangements, and finally they discover how to use bulb and battery holders to keep things connected.

◆Time management

One class period (40–60 minutes) should be enough time to complete the activity and discuss the results.

◆Preparation

Cut the wire into 20-cm lengths. If you are using plastic-coated or enamel-coated wire, remove about 4 cm of plastic or enamel from each end of the wire so that 4 cm of bare wire shows at each end. Beware— there is a clear enamel-coated wire that is easily mistaken for bare copper wire. The enamel coating on this wire (like the plastic coating on other wires) is a nonconductor and must be scraped or sanded off the ends of the wire before the wire can be used as a conductor of electricity.

Test the bulbs and batteries to make sure they are in working order. Save burned out bulbs and dead batteries for later use.

Assemble the battery holders from one thick rubber band and two Fahnestock clips. The rubber band should be just big enough to fit around the D cell lengthwise. Stretch the rubber band and slide it between the spring tab and the loop on the Fahnestock clip. You might have to bend the spring tab up a little to get the rubber band through. Have some students help you with this.

The Fahnestock clip works by pressing the spring tab down, inserting the end of wire in the loop, and releasing the tab so it springs upward and holds the wire tightly in the loop. If the wire is not held securely, remove the wire and bend the spring tab away from the loop and try again.

Warn students that the bulbs need not be tightly screwed into the sockets. All that is necessary is that the socket parts touch the thread and bump parts of the bulb. Excessive tightening will bend some sockets out of shape.

◆Suggestions for further study

Invent new ways to securely hold wires to batteries and bulbs.

Discover a way to light two bulbs with two wires and one battery. You'll need help holding the objects.

Set up an arrangement of two wires, one battery in its holder, and one bulb in its holder that looks like it should light the bulb but does not. Present this arrangement to another group of students and challenge them to find out what's wrong without touching the arrangement.

◆Answers

1 and 2.   The arrangements which light the bulb are 1, 5, and 6. The arrangements which do not light the bulb are 2, 3, and 4.

3.   Two different two-wire arrangements that light the bulb are:

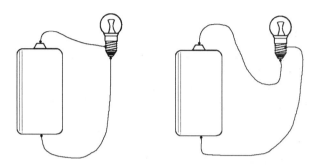

4.   The battery and bulb holder can be used in the following way to light the bulb.

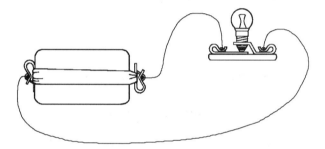

ACTIVITY 17 WORKSHEET

Just Passing Through: Conductors and Nonconductors

◆Background

In this activity, you will first get more experience with using sockets in electrical arrangements. Next, based on the notion that electricity passes through some objects, you will invent and use an electrical device that tells you whether or not electricity is passing through a material.

◆Objectives

To gain a more thorough understanding of how sockets work or fail to work in an electrical arrangement
To construct and use an electrical device for testing whether or not materials allow electrical charges to move through them
To identify which kinds of materials are conductors (allow movement of electrical charges) and which kinds of materials are nonconductors (do not allow movement of electrical charges)

◆Procedure

1. Without testing the arrangements first, circle the number on the battery of those arrangements that will light the bulb.

2. Very carefully look at each arrangement below and then use the materials to test each arrangement. Write "light" by those bulbs that are found to actually light. Write "no light" by those bulbs that do not light. Be able to explain why the no light arrangements do not light.

Materials

For each group:
• two #48 flashlight bulbs
• five 20-centimeter wires: four pieces of #22 plastic-coated wire with plastic removed from the ends
• one #24 enamel-coated wire with 4 cm of enamel scraped or sanded from each end
• two bulb holders or sockets
• one "D" battery (dry cell)
• one battery holder (2 Fahnestock clips on a rubber band)
• assorted conducting and nonconducting materials

Include pencil "lead," metal paper clip, piece of paper, and silvery Mylar if you can find it.

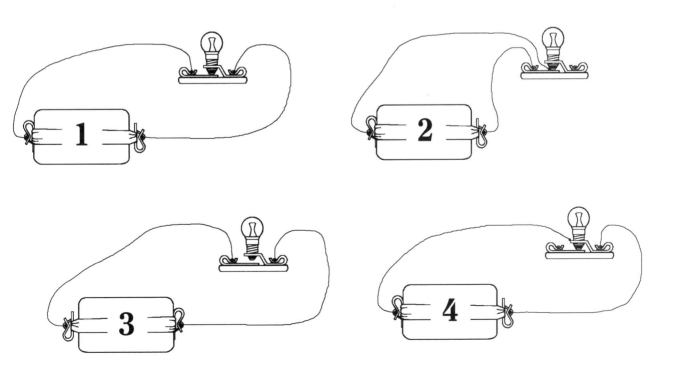

3. Under certain conditions electricity moves from one place to another. It moves easily through some materials but does not move easily through other materials. Later on we will describe what is moving, why and how it moves, and why it moves through some materials and not others.

Challenge: Using 3 wires, 1 bulb in its holder, and 1 battery in its holder, invent an electrical device that tells you whether or not electricity passes through an object. Test your device with a metal paper clip (conductor) and a piece of paper (nonconductor).

a. Draw a picture of your testing device.

b. Put your device to use by testing a number of different objects or parts of objects. Write the names of the objects in the column on the left in the table below and then identify them as conductors or nonconductors on the right.

c. Look at the conductors and nonconductors in the table below.
Conductors generally are (metals or non-metals)_____.

Nonconductors generally are (metals or non-metals)_____.

Table

Objects	Conductor (C) or Nonconductor (NC)
1.	C or NC
2.	C or NC
3.	C or NC
4.	C or NC
5.	C or NC
6.	C or NC
7.	C or NC
8.	C or NC
9. The plastic covering on a wire	C or NC
10. The enameled portion (middle) of an enameled piece of wire	C or NC
11. The scraped or sanded ends of an enameled piece of wire	C or NC
12. The thread part of a bulb	C or NC
13. The bump at the base of a bulb	C or NC
14. The dark material between the bump and the thread at the base of a bulb	C or NC
15. The plastic or ceramic base of the bulb holder or socket	C or NC
16. That part of the bulb holder which touches the thread of the bulb	C or NC

GUIDE TO ACTIVITY 17

Just Passing Through: Conductors and Nonconductors

◆What is happening?

In this activity, students get more experience using sockets in electrical arrangements. They discover that the bulb must be screwed in far enough so that the bump on the end of the bulb touches the conductor. Next, based on the notion that electricity passes through some objects, the students invent and use an electrical device that tells them whether or not electricity is passing through a material. They determine which parts of bulbs, sockets, and wires are conductors and which parts are nonconductors. The students conclude from their tests that conductors of electricity usually are metals and that nonconductors are non-metals such as plastic, wood, paper, rubber, and glass.

◆Time management

One class period (40–60 minutes) should be enough time to complete the activity and discuss the results.

◆Preparation

You can use materials from previous activities, but you will likely have to cut more wire. Remember, about 4 cm of plastic or enamel must be removed from the ends of the plastic- or enamel-covered wires. Have students help in acquiring other assorted materials.

◆Suggestions for further study

Find a material that looks like a conductor but that is a nonconductor. Find a material that looks like a nonconductor but that is a conductor.
    Test a strong salt solution to see if it is a conductor. Also, try vinegar.

◆Answers

1 and 2.   Only arrangement 1 lights. Arrangement 2 does not light because neither end of the battery is connected to the thread part of the bulb. Arrangement 3 does not light because the bump of the bulb does not touch the part of the holder that is connected to one end of the battery. Arrangement 4 does not light because the bump of the bulb is not connected to one end of the battery.

3a. The conductor testing device should look like the following. Some students may leave out one of the wires and touch the object to be tested directly to the battery or the bulb holder.

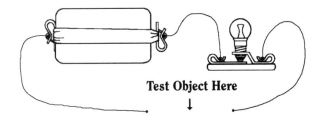

Test Object Here
↓

b. 1–8 Various conducting and nonconducting objects

9. The plastic covering on a wire	NC
10. The enameled portion (middle) of an enameled piece of wire	NC
11. The scraped or sanded ends of an enameled piece of wire	C
12. The thread part of a bulb	C
13. The bump at the base of a bulb	C
14. The dark material between the bump and the thread at the base of a bulb	NC
15. The plastic or ceramic base of the bulb holder or socket	NC
16. That part of the bulb holder which touches the thread of the bulb	C

c. Conductors generally are <u>metals</u>. Nonconductors generally are <u>non-metals</u>.

ACTIVITY 18 WORKSHEET

Light Bulb Anatomy, Circuits, and Switches

◆Background

Electricity follows a pathway of conductors as it travels from one end of the battery to the other end. In this activity, you will explore the anatomy of the light bulb and discover the pathway of conductors through the bulb. You will discover what happens to the pathway when a bulb is "burned out." You will learn about closed and open circuits and will examine some circuits to determine whether they are open or closed. Finally you will invent switches that will open and close circuits.

◆Objective

To describe the pathway of conductors in a light bulb
To define and apply the concepts of open and closed circuits

◆Procedure

1. The bump on the bottom of the bulb and the metal threaded area around the base of the bulb must be touched (directly or indirectly through a wire) to the ends of a battery to light the bulb. What is inside the bulb and what does the inside have to do with the thread and bump? Carefully observe a bulb. What is that metal bump at the top of the threaded area, next to the glass?

a. Circle the drawing below which best shows the wiring inside a bulb. Hint: The correct wiring inside a bulb will allow electricity to move through the bulb from one end of the battery to the other end.

Light a bulb with one wire and one battery and notice that there is only one part of the bulb which gives off light. The part that glows is called the filament—a very thin wire which is often made out of a metal called tungsten. The filament is a conductor of electricity. When enough electricity flows through the filament, the filament gets hot and gives off light.

b. In each of the following drawings, add in the wires inside the base of the bulb. Then, with either a colored pencil or a wiggly line, mark the complete pathway of conductors from one end of the battery through the wires in the bulb to the other end of the battery.

Materials

For each group:

• one #48 flashlight bulb

• two 20-centimeter wires—#22 plastic-coated wire with plastic removed from the ends.

• two "D" batteries (dry cells)

For the class:

• Assorted materials for building switches: poster board, paper clips, transparent tape, brass fasteners, aluminum foil, rubber bands, aluminum pie pans from which pieces of aluminum might be cut, etc.

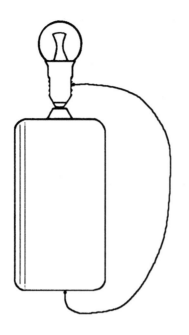
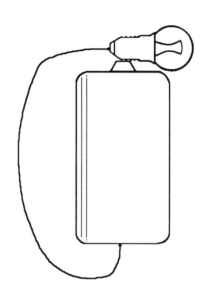

2. Circuits can be open or closed. Whenever there is a complete (uninterrupted) path of conductors from one end of the battery to the other end of the battery we call the arrangement a *closed* circuit. If the path is incomplete, then we call it an *open* circuit. The word "circuit" comes from a Latin word that means "a going around."

a. Write "closed" by each of the following closed circuits and write "open" by each of the following open circuits. Set up and test these circuits and write "light" by those circuits which light the bulb.

1
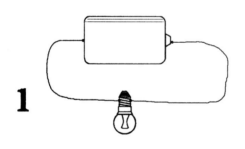

2
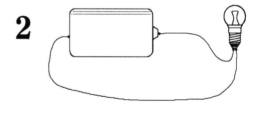

3
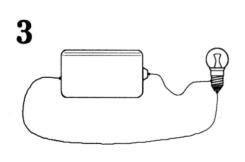

4
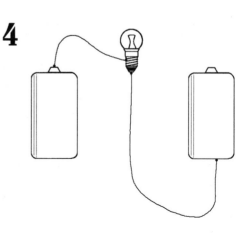

b. Write the numbers of the circuits above which are closed but do not light a bulb. _____

c. Is it possible to have a closed circuit and not have a lighted bulb? If yes, how?

_____

_____

d. Which circuit on page 94 shows that a closed circuit is not formed when the ends of different batteries are touched? _____
This indicates that for electricity to flow, there must be a complete path, even through the battery (or batteries, if the batteries are connected top to bottom).

e. Look closely at the bulb in the following drawing. Is the circuit open or closed?_____

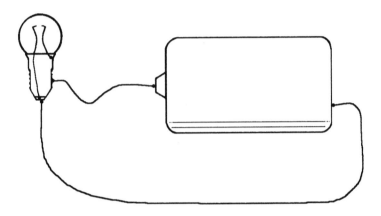

f. What do you think happens when a bulb burns out or stops lighting, even though it is properly hooked up to wires and a good battery?

_____

_____

3. A switch is a device that can easily open and close a circuit. One type is a knife switch. When the bar or blade is down, the circuit is closed (creating a continuous path of conductors) and the bulb lights. When the bar or blade is up, the path of conductors is broken and the circuit is open and the light goes out.
    Another type is the switch used in homes. A household switch should never be investigated unless it is completely removed from all wires. A somewhat simplified side view of a household switch is shown on the next page. Notice that when the plastic "switch" is down, it holds a springy strip of brass away from the contact point so there could be no flow of electricity between the wires. When the plastic switch is up, it allows the springy strip of brass to make contact at the contact point and there is now a closed circuit of conductors.
    One light can be controlled by two switches. You may have noticed that in your home two switches can control one light. You walk into a room, switch on the light, walk across the room and turn off the same light from a different switch. How is it possible for two switches to control one light?

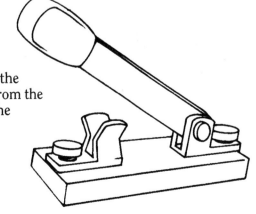

Knife Switch

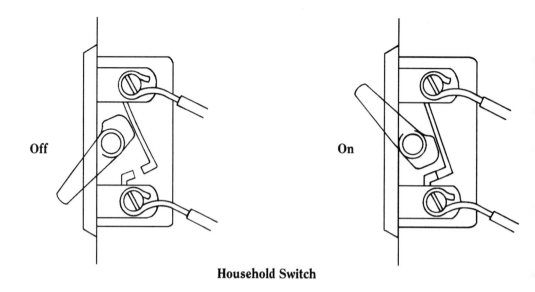

Household Switch

The following circuit shows two switches, A and B. Either switch can be in the up (1) or down (2) position. When a switch is down (position 2), the common point is connected by a conductor to point 2. When a switch is up (position 1) the common point is connected to point 1.

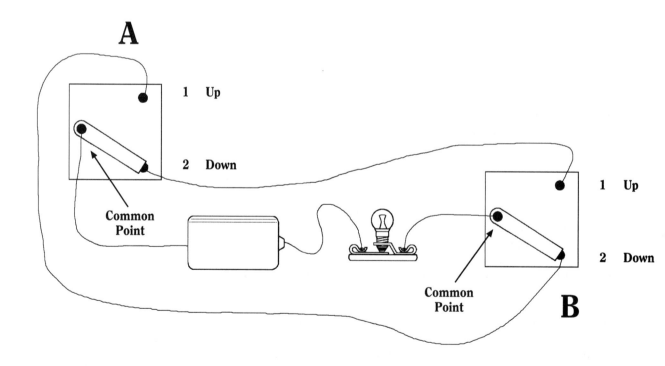

a. Consider the following up and down positions of switches A and B and decide whether or not the bulb will light.

Switch A	Switch B	Will the bulb light?
UP (1)	UP (1)	
UP (1)	DOWN (2)	
DOWN (2)	UP (1)	
DOWN (2)	DOWN (2)	

b. When B is up, is it possible to turn the light on and off with switch A?_____

c. When B is down, is it possible to turn the light on and off with switch A?_____

d. When B is up, what position—up (1) or down (2)—must A be in to turn the light on?_____

GUIDE TO ACTIVITY 18

Light Bulb Anatomy, Circuits, and Switches

◆What is happening?

In this activity, students explore the anatomy of the light bulb and discover the pathway of conductors (including the filament) through the bulb. They see the bulb as nothing more than a device for holding and protecting that fragile piece of wire called the filament. Students learn that a burned out bulb merely has a broken filament. Students learn and apply the concepts of open and closed circuits and then study different kinds of switches.

◆Time management

Two class periods of about 40–60 minutes each should be more than enough time to complete the activity and discuss the results. The second class period may start with switches. If more time is available during the second class, students may be challenged to invent switches described in "Suggestions for further study."

◆Preparation

In addition to preparing and checking wires and batteries, you may wish to:

1. Show students the insides of a couple of regular household light switches. To get at the inside of some switches, you will have to drill out the rivets which hold some of the parts together.

2. Set up a demonstration model of the two-way switches used in part 2a. (one light controlled by two switches).

3. Take apart a flashlight bulb. To do this wrap the glass part of a bulb with a cloth, very gently grip the cloth and glass with a pair of pliers, and twist the glass free of the threaded part of the bulb. The glass is lightly cemented into the threaded part of the bulb. Show the students how the wires leave the glass and go to the thread and to the bump.

Short circuits are really "easy" circuits for the electricity to follow in moving from one end of the battery to the other end. The connecting wire provides an easy pathway. The filaments in the bulb provide "difficult" pathways. Electricity moves very easily along the easy or short circuits, eventually heating up the wires and running down the battery. See the safety note at left.

● Caution—When students test the circuits in step 2, they will create short circuits for arrangements 1 and 2. The wires might get hot and the battery may warm up. Warn students not to keep these arrangements hooked up for more than 30 seconds.

◆Suggestions for further study

Design, build, and demonstrate a "one finger, jiggle proof, walk away" switch. "One finger" means that the switch can be turned on and off with just one finger. "Jiggle proof" means that when the switch is on or off it keeps the circuit open or closed in spite of being jiggled. "Walk away" means that you can walk away and the switch will stay on or off.

Design, build, and demonstrate a "press and hold on" switch. "Press and hold on" means that the switch stays on (closes the circuit) only while the switch is being pressed with your finger. This switch opens the circuit when your finger is removed.

Design a tilt-a-switch. This switch would turn on or off depending upon which way the switch is turned, tipped, or tilted.

Design a "hair-trigger, touchy, twitchy" switch. This switch would close a circuit and turn on a light or a buzzer even if it is gently touched.

Examine the switch in a flashlight to see how it opens and closes a circuit.

Examine a household light bulb to see how its construction compares to the construction of a flashlight bulb.

◆Answers

1a. The third bulb from the left shows the correct wiring inside the light bulb.

b.   The drawings should look like the following:

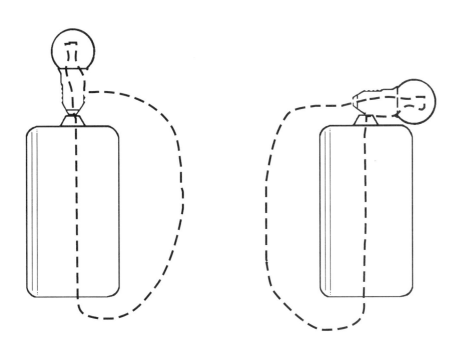

2a. Circuits 1, 2, and 3 should be labeled closed circuits. In circuit 1, the filament, which is a conductor, is part of a path of conductors. However, the bulb in circuit 1 does not light because the path the electricity takes does not go through the filament of the bulb. A similar situation is shown in circuit 2. Circuit 4 should be labeled open because there is no complete closed path (see 2d). The only circuit that lights the bulb is circuit 3.

b.   Circuits 1 and 2 are closed but do not light the bulb. See the above explanation.

c.   Yes. All you need is a complete path of conductors to create a closed circuit. Closed circuits may or may not include a filament which glows when electricity passes through it.

d.   Circuit 4 shows how a closed circuit is not formed when the ends of different batteries are touched.

e.   The circuit is open. The filament is broken and there no longer is a complete path of conductors from one end of the battery to the other.

f.   When a bulb "burns out" it no longer lights because the filament is broken. Over time, a glowing filament gets thin and brittle and eventually breaks. Also, a filament may get too hot and melt.

3a. The correct responses are:

Switch A	Switch B	Will the bulb light?
UP (1)	UP (1)	**NO**
UP (1)	DOWN (2)	**YES**
DOWN (2)	UP (1)	**YES**
DOWN (2)	DOWN (2)	**NO**

b.   When B is up, is it possible to turn the light on and off with switch A? <u>Yes</u>

c.   When B is down, is it possible to turn the light on and off with switch A? <u>Yes</u>

d.   When B is up, what position—up (1) or down (2)—must A be in to turn the light on? <u>Down (2)</u>

ACTIVITY 19 WORKSHEET

Series Circuits and Resistance:
All for One and One for All

◆Background

Sometimes it is easy to follow a pathway and sometimes it is more difficult. If the path is smooth and wide, you can travel at a rather fast pace. If the path is bumpy and narrow, you might travel at a slower pace. A similar situation holds for electricity as it moves along the pathways of conductors. Sometimes it is easy for electricity to flow and sometimes it is more difficult. In this activity you will discover a kind of circuit that makes flow difficult, and be introduced to the concept of electrical resistance.

◆Objective

To construct a series circuit and to describe what is meant by electrical resistance

◆Procedure

1. When one Christmas tree light goes out, why do they all go out? Before tackling the challenge, use the materials to set up and explore the following basic circuit. Notice the brightness of the bulb.

a. On the drawing below use a colored pencil or a wiggly line and draw the path of conductors from one end of the battery through the bulb and back to the other end of the battery.

Materials

For each group:
- three #48 bulbs
- three bulb holders
- one "D" battery
- one battery holder (two Fahnestock clips on a rubber band)
- four 20-centimeter wires (#22 plastic-coated wire with plastic removed from the ends or #24 enamel-coated wire with the enamel scraped or sanded from the ends)
- one #2 pencil sharpened at both ends with 1 cm of "lead" exposed at the middle
- optional piece of #32 nichrome wire (1–1.5 meters long)

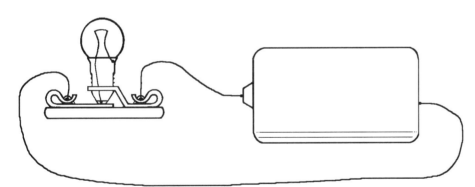

b. **Challenge:** With three wires, two bulbs in their holders, and one battery in its holder, create a circuit of two lighted bulbs so that when either bulb is unscrewed from its socket and goes out, the other bulb goes out. Only two objects (wires or parts of bulb holders) can touch the battery. Draw your circuit below.

c. Why does the one bulb go out when the other bulb is unscrewed from its socket?

_____

_____

d. When both bulbs in your invented circuit are on, how does the brightness of the bulbs compare to the brightness of the bulb in step 1 above?

_____

_____

2. The circuit you invented to solve this problem is called a series circuit. There is only one pathway of conductors from one end of the battery to the other end, and that pathway is through both bulbs.

In a series circuit, if one bulb does not light, none of the others will light. All work or none work. All for one and one for all.

a. Assume you have a two-bulb series circuit and electricity is flowing and the bulbs are lighted. What would happen if one of the bulbs burned out (its filament broke)?

_____

_____

_____

_____

b. You have developed a two-bulb series circuit. Now add another bulb and its socket to make a three-bulb series circuit. How does the brightness of the bulbs in a three-bulb series circuit compare to the brightness of bulbs in a two-bulb series circuit?

_____

_____

c. In general, what happens to bulb brightness as you increase the number of bulbs in a series circuit?

_____

_____

3a. In a series circuit, if one object in the series is turned off or burns out (a break in the conductors), then none objects in the circuit function. Are the electrical devices in your home connected in series? Why or why not?

_____

_____

4. You have noticed that as you add bulbs in series, the brightness of bulbs decrease. The brightness of bulbs is, in part, an indication of the rate of flow of electricity through the circuit. If the bulbs are dim, then the flow of electricity is less. If the bulbs are bright, then the flow of electricity is greater. One of the reasons the amount of electricity can vary is because of the amount of resistance in the circuit. Greater resistance results in lesser flow and lesser resistance results in greater flow, provided the push from the battery is the same.

The movement of electricity in a circuit would be like you walking along a path. You would likely walk slower along a narrow, rough path which has many obstacles (more resistance) and faster along a wide, smooth path which has few obstacles (less resistance).

Each bulb, and particularly the filament in each bulb, provides resistance to the flow of electricity. When one bulb is in a closed circuit, the bulb provides some resistance, but a lot of electricity still flows and the bulb is bright. When two bulbs are connected in series, each one adds resistance to the flow and the flow is less at all parts in the circuit. When three bulbs are connected in series, the resistance to the flow is even greater than what it is for the two-bulb circuit.

When you created a two-bulb series circuit, were both bulbs the same brightness? _____ Check your answer by setting up a two-bulb series circuit. Make sure you have the same kind of bulb in each holder or socket.

5. Your answer to the last question may raise other questions. If electrons are leaving one end of the battery, traveling through the two bulbs, and entering the other end of the battery, why can't you see one bulb light before the other? Furthermore, why are both bulbs in a series circuit equally dim? Why don't the bulbs become dimmer further down the line in a series circuit? To help answer these questions, imagine a train running on a circular track. The train is so long that its engine is touching the back of the last car.

a. If the brakes are applied on one car of the train to slow it down, what happens to the other cars?

_____

b. How might this be like resistance and electrons in a circuit?

_____

_____

The train model illustrates another property of electrical flow. Because the cars are connected, the instant one car is moved, all cars move. The instant a circuit is closed, electrons are moving at once in all the bulbs and wires of the circuit. The instant electrons leave the negative end of the battery (the flat end), electrons enter the positive end of the battery (the bump end). When a series circuit is closed, electrons are moving in the second bulb at the same time as they are moving in the first bulb. One bulb is no brighter than the other and the first bulb does not appear to light before the second.

6. Some materials have a tremendous resistance to the flow of electricity. These materials are nonconductors or insulators such as plastic, wood, rubber, glass, etc. While conductors allow electricity to flow, they differ in how much they resist. Copper and aluminum, common metals used in wiring, provide more resistance than does silver. Tungsten, which is used in bulb filaments, and nichrome, which is an alloy of iron, nickel, and chromium, have greater resistances than copper and aluminum. See the table below. Besides the kind of material, there are other factors that determine the amount of resistance.

Conductors/Insulators

Conductors
Silver   Better
Copper
Gold
Aluminum
Calcium
Tungsten
Nickel
Iron
Platinum
Chromium   Worse

Insulators
Better   Paraffin
                                              Sulfur
                                              Mica
                                              Rubber
                                              Beeswax
                                              Glass
                                   Wood (hard, dried)
                                       Petroleum Jelly
                                              Marble
                                        Manila Paper
                                          Soapstone
                                              Ivory
Worse   Slate

Set up a circuit like the one shown below. Observe the brightness of the bulb when the two wires are touched together.

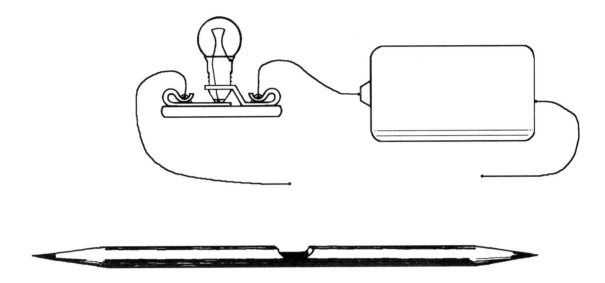

7. Next observe the brightness of the bulb as the electricity travels different distances through pencil "lead" (graphite). Observe bulb brightness when the electricity travels:
• the thickness of the lead at one end of the pencil
• half a pencil length
• the entire length of a pencil

a. How is the length of graphite through which electricity passes related to resistance?

_____

_____

The relationship holds for other materials as well. If you have about 1.5 meters of #32 nichrome wire, use the set up described above and observe how resistance changes bulb brightness as the electricity travels through different lengths of the wire. Stretch the wire out in a straight line. Touch one of the circuit wires to one end of the nichrome wire. Touch the other circuit wire to the nichrome wire at different distances along the wire.

Two other factors that influence resistance are temperature and the thickness of the conductor. Generally, conductors at higher temperatures have greater resistances. Thin conductors have more resistance than thick conductors.

b. Using some of the following terms ("copper, tungsten, silver, short, long, thick, thin, hot, and cold"), describe a conductor that has the greatest resistance and a conductor that has the least resistance to the flow of electricity.

_____

_____

_____

_____

GUIDE TO ACTIVITY 19

Series Circuits and Resistance: All for One and One for All

◆What is happening?

In this activity students will create a series circuit. They will use ideas of open and closed circuits to explain why when one bulb in a series circuit goes out the other bulbs in the same circuit go out. The students will be introduced to the concept of electrical resistance. They will learn how the kind of material and how the length, thickness, and temperature of a conductor are related to electrical resistance. Also, students are introduced to the ideas that electrons flow in conductors, that the rate of electron flow is influenced by resistance, and that bulb brightness is related to the rate of electron flow.

Students should learn that the rate of electron flow is the same at all points along the path of conductors from one end of the battery to the other end. Resistance at any one point in the circuit affects electron flow at all points along the circuit. It is as if the electrons flowing through the conductors are somehow linked (being of like charge, they repel one another) so that if resistance is applied at one point, all points are affected because of the linking.

◆Time management

Two class periods of about 40–60 minutes might be necessary for the completion of this activity. The series circuit might be explored during the first and resistance might be explored during the second.

◆Preparation

Most of the bulbs, wires, and batteries that will be used in this activity have been used in previous activities and might need checking.

If you have #32 nichrome wire and intend to use it in this activity, you will need to cut 1.5 meters of wire for each group.

In this activity students will investigate how the length of pencil "lead" (actually graphite) through which electricity passes influences resistance (the longer the length, the greater the resistance). Conveniently, wooden pencils provide the graphite nicely protected in the wooden jacket. All you need to do is cut away some of the wood. Start with a new #2 pencil and cut off the metal top which holds the eraser. Sharpen both ends of the pencil. With a utility knife cut away wood in the center of the pencil to expose about one centimeter of graphite. Try not to cut into the graphite. Do not cut through the graphite. If test wires are touched at each end, electricity has to run the full length of the graphite. If the test wires touch one end and the middle, then the electricity has to run half a pencil length. If the test wires do not touch each other but do touch the graphite across the sharpened end of the pencil, then the electricity will have the shortest distance to travel through the graphite.

◆Suggestions for further study

Create a "people analogy" that uses people to show how electrons flow in a series circuit. Include "resistance" and the "push" from the battery.

Some Christmas tree lights are arranged in a series. When one bulb goes out, all the others go out. Why do you think manufacturers of such lights would prefer to use a series circuit?

Graph the relationship between the length of nichrome wire the electricity passes through and the brightness of a bulb in the circuit. To measure the brightness, see how many thicknesses of paper it takes to block out the light coming from the bulb in the following way. Drill a six-millimeter hole in the bottom of a black 35 mm film canister. Place the opening of the canister near the bulb. Put a folded piece of paper between the opening and the light bulb. Look through the hole in the bottom of the canister to see if you see light from the bulb getting through the paper. If you do, fold the paper to get one more thickness of paper through which the light must pass. The number of folds of paper it takes to block the light from a bulb is a measure of bulb brightness.

◆Answers

1a. A drawing which shows the path of electricity from one end of the battery through the circuit to the other end of the battery might be:

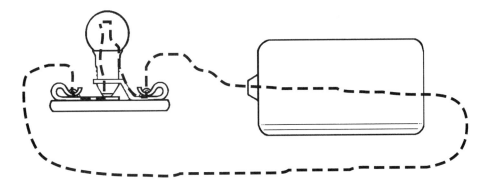

b. A circuit that solves the problem might be:

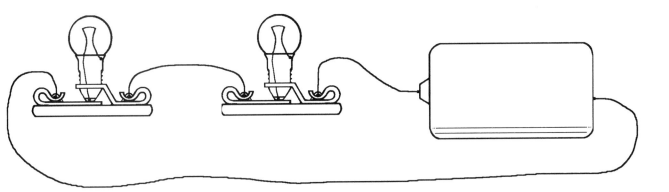

c. When one bulb is unscrewed from its socket, there is no longer a complete path of conductors from one end of the battery to the other. There is a gap between the bump on the bottom of the unscrewed bulb and the metal part of the bulb holder or socket.

d. When two bulbs are lighted in the circuit, neither bulb is as bright as a single bulb that is lighted by a battery.

2a. If the filament in one of the bulbs burned out or broke, the other bulb would go out also. The filament is part of the path of conductors and if there is a gap in the filament, then the circuit is open and the electricity stops flowing.

b. The bulbs in a three-bulb series circuit are not as bright as the bulbs in a two-bulb series circuit.

c. As the number of bulbs in a series circuit increases, the brightness of all the bulbs in the circuit decreases.

3a. The electrical devices in homes are not connected in series because when one device is turned off or burns out other devices can continue to operate.

4. When two bulbs were connected in series, the bulbs were of equal brightness and were not as bright (each) as a bulb in a one-bulb circuit.

5a. The other cars slow down also.

b. Resistance at any one point in the circuit affects electron flow at all points along the circuit. The electrons are like the cars in the train, so that resistance applied at any point in the circuit reduces electron flow at all points in the circuit.

7a. When different lengths of pencil "lead" were tested for resistance, the bulb became dimmer for the greater lengths. The greater the length, the greater the electrical resistance. The same relationship is observed using nichrome wire instead of graphite.

b. A short, thick, and cold piece of silver would provide the least resistance. A long, hot, and thin piece of tungsten would provide the greatest resistance.

ACTIVITY 20 WORKSHEET

Parallel Circuits: Sometimes Short and Always Independent

◆Background

If one bulb in a series circuit goes out, all bulbs in the circuit go out. Obviously, this is not the best design for a circuit to use in homes—to run one thing, all things would have to be running. In this activity, you will make a new kind of circuit and this circuit will be the kind used in homes. You will also be introduced to a misnamed circuit called the short circuit—a rather dangerous circuit which has destroyed many homes.

◆Objectives

To create a parallel (independent) circuit and explain how it works in terms of open and closed circuits
To identify short circuits as circuits with very little resistance and a likely path for electricity to follow

◆Procedure

1a. **Challenge:** Make an independent circuit like the kind used in homes—Using four wires, two bulbs in their holders, and one battery in its holder, create a two-bulb circuit so that when either bulb is unscrewed from its holder and goes out, the other bulb stays lighted. The battery can be touched only by two objects (wires or parts of bulb holders). Draw your circuit below.

Materials

For each group:
• two #48 bulbs
• two bulb holders
• one "D" battery (dry cell)
• one battery holder (two Fahnestock clips on a rubber band)
• six 20-centimeter wires (#22 plastic-coated wire with plastic removed from the ends or #24 enamel-coated wire with the enamel scraped or sanded from the ends)

b. Why does the one bulb stay lighted when the other bulb is unscrewed from its socket and goes out?

_____

_____

c. In the following drawing add the wires to show this new invented circuit. Notice that one bulb is unscrewed in its socket and will not light. The other bulb should be lighted. Use a colored pencil or a "wiggly" line to show the path of electricity from one end of the battery through the wires, socket parts, and lighted bulb to the other end of the battery.

Off

On

The circuit you have invented is called a parallel circuit. In this circuit, each bulb has it own direct or independent path to the battery. When one bulb is unscrewed from its socket, the other bulb will still be lighted because it has its own independent path to the ends of the battery. This is the kind of circuit used in wiring homes. With the parallel circuit, you can turn on or off any electrical device regardless of whether or not the rest of the devices are on or off.

If homes were wired with series circuits rather than with parallel circuits, all devices would have to be turned on before any one device would work and if one device was turned off all devices would go off.

2.   Write a "p" by each of the following circuits you think is a parallel circuit. Build each circuit and see if it is a parallel circuit. In a parallel circuit only the bulb which is unscrewed will go out; the others will stay lighted.

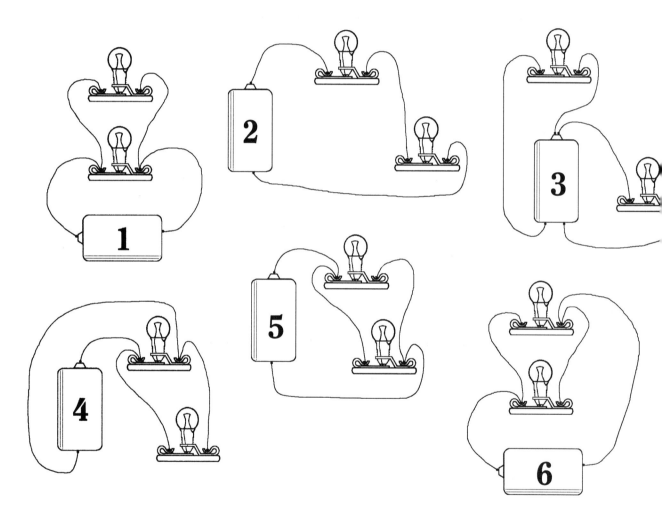

Why is the word "parallel" used to describe these circuits? The word parallel is often used to describe lines that are alongside one another and are the same distance apart.

The bulbs and wires in a parallel circuit do not have to be equal distances apart, but like parallel lines, the independent circuits lie alongside of one another, each with its own independent connection to the battery. Arrangements #1 and #4 above best show these side by side, independent circuits.

3. Create a one-bulb circuit and observe the brightness of the bulb.
Create a two-bulb *parallel* circuit and observe the brightness of the bulbs.
Create a two-bulb *series* circuit and observe the brightness of the bulbs.

a. If the bulb in the one-bulb circuit is considered "bright," then the bulbs in the two-bulb parallel circuit would be described as

_____.

b. The bulbs in the two-bulb series circuit (compared to those in the parallel circuit) would be described as _____.

c. Are the bulbs within each circuit equally bright?

_____

d. Explain why the bulbs in the series circuit are not the same brightness as the bulbs in the parallel circuit.

_____

_____

_____

_____

e. Would a battery last longer as part of a two-bulb parallel circuit or as part of a two-bulb series circuit? Explain your answer.

_____

_____

_____

_____

4a. Challenge: Build a one-bulb circuit. Without unscrewing the bulb from its holder and without removing wires from the battery or bulb holder, use a third wire to make the bulb go out. Do not leave this third wire attached for very long. Draw a picture below showing how you solved the problem.

b. When the third wire is attached and the bulb is out, does the third wire make a closed circuit?_____

c. Explain why the bulb goes out when the third wire is attached.

_____

_____

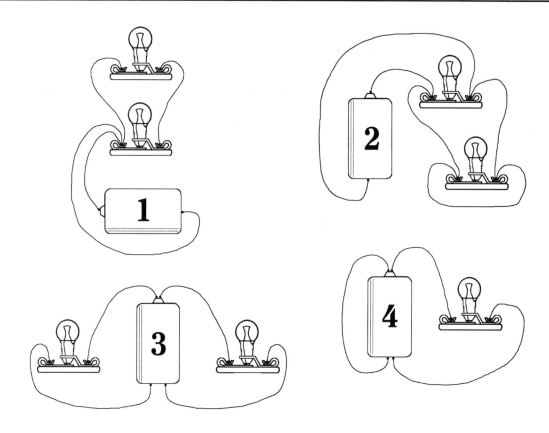

5a. Without testing the circuits first, write an "L" by the arrangements above in which at least one bulb will light.

b.   Test each of these circuits. Do not leave any of these circuits hooked up for more than 15 seconds. Write "lights" by those bulbs which actually light.

Electricity is both "smart" and "lazy." There will be more electricity flowing along the easier paths of a circuit than along more difficult paths. In other words, more electricity flows along paths of lesser resistance. To solve the problem in step 4a you used the third wire to create a very easy path for the electricity to follow. More electricity flowed along the easier path (through the third wire) than along the path of greater resistance through the bulb. In three of the arrangements above, there are also easy paths for the electricity to follow. Use either a colored pencil or a "wiggly" line to identify the easy circuit in each of three arrangements above.

The easy circuits which you created and identified in step 5a and 5b are traditionally called "short circuits." In arrangement #2 above, more electricity flows through the longest (outside) circuit, that is along the wires around, not through, the bulbs. This circuit provides the least resistance and is called a short circuit. Basically, short circuits are easy circuits regardless of how long they are.

These easy circuits got the name short because they often are short. The easy and short circuit shown here is often the kind of short circuit which occurs in homes. In homes, a short circuit might occur if the insulation between two wires in an electrical cord breaks down and allows the two wires to touch.

The electricity takes the easy path or short cut before ever getting to the lamp or toaster or hair dryer or whatever. These easy paths provide very little resistance to the flow of electricity. Consequently, most of the electricity (electrons) travels through them and the circuits heat up. If the wires get too hot, a fire will be started. In homes, there are fuses or circuit breakers that cause an opening in the circuit when the electrical flow becomes so great that wires might heat to the point of starting a fire.

GUIDE TO ACTIVITY 20

Parallel Circuits: Sometimes Short and Always Independent

◆What is happening?

In this activity, students solve a problem and in doing so create the parallel circuit. They see how each of the electrical pathways in a parallel circuit has its own access to the battery. Students learn that the parallel circuit is the kind of circuit used in homes. They observe that the bulbs in a two-bulb parallel circuit are about as bright as the bulb in a single bulb circuit and brighter than the bulbs in a two-bulb series circuit. Because the bulbs in a parallel circuit are independent and have their own access to the battery, the resistance in each bulb's branch of the circuit is about the same as it would be in the bulb in a single bulb circuit.

Students invent a short circuit in the process of solving a problem. They learn that a short circuit isn't always short in length but is always an easy pathway for electricity to follow. The danger of short circuits in homes is subsequently described. Students come to understand that the rate of electrical flow is greatest along the paths of least resistance.

◆Time management

One class period (40–60 minutes) should be enough time to complete the activity and discuss the results.

◆Preparation

No special preparation is necessary.

◆Suggestions for further study

Create a circuit that has both parallel and series components. In other words, try creating a circuit in which at least one bulb is bright and one bulb is dim. Allow only two wires to touch the battery. Make sure you use the same kind of bulbs.

Assume that during the night the circuits in your home are changed from parallel circuits to one large series circuit. Describe what would happen in the morning as everyone gets ready for work and school.

It is possible to buy strings of Christmas tree lights that are arranged in parallel. Try drawing a string of four lights showing the parallel arrangement. Why would you, as the owner who must replace burned-out lights, prefer a parallel arrangement of the lights to a series arrangement? Why might manufacturers of Christmas tree lights prefer to make series arrangements?

◆Answers

1a. The following circuits will solve the problem:

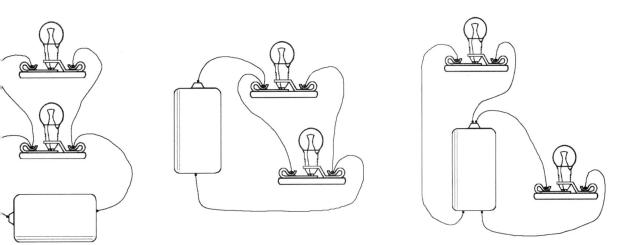

b. The one bulb stays lighted even though the other is unscrewed from its socket because the lighted bulb has its own pathway to the battery and is part of a closed circuit.

c. The following drawing shows a parallel circuit with one bulb lighted.

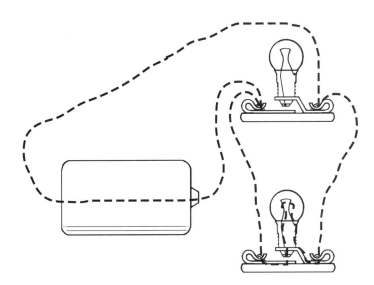

The dotted line shows the path of electricity through the lighted bulb.

2. All but circuit #2 are parallel circuits.

3a. Each of the two bulbs in a parallel circuit are about as bright as a bulb in a single-bulb circuit.

b. Both bulbs in a two-bulb series circuit are dim compared to the bulbs in a two-bulb parallel circuit.

c. Yes, the bulbs within each circuit are equally bright.

d. The bulbs in a two-bulb parallel circuit are about as bright as the bulb in a single-bulb circuit and brighter than the bulbs in a two-bulb series circuit. Because the bulbs in a parallel circuit are independent and have their own access to the battery, the resistance in each bulb's branch of the circuit is about the same as it would be in the bulb in a single-bulb circuit. The bulbs in a series circuit each contribute to the resistance and together provide more resistance than one bulb. In the series circuit, the electricity has to overcome two sources of resistance while getting from one end of the battery to the other end. Therefore, the electrical flow is slow and the bulbs are dim.

e.   A battery would last longer as part of a two-bulb series circuit than part of a two-bulb parallel circuit. The parallel circuit keeps two bulbs brightly lighted while the series circuit keeps two bulbs dimly lighted. In the same amount of time, the battery in the parallel circuit would give up more energy and would wear out faster.

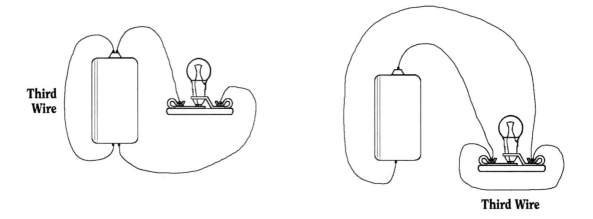

4a. The drawings above show how to put out the bulb with the third wire.

b.   Yes, there is a closed circuit through the third wire.

c.   The bulb goes out because most of the electricity goes through the third wire rather than through the bulb.

5.   Only the lights in arrangement #3 will light.

ACTIVITY 21 WORKSHEET

The Power Structure and Cell Anatomy

Materials

For each group:

•one #48 bulb in its socket

•two D or C batteries (dry cells) in their battery holders

•six wires

•two switches—each made from a 5 cm X 5 cm piece of thin cardboard and two metal paper clips

◆Background

Just as we can have circuits with more than one bulb, we can also have circuits with more than one battery. What happens to bulb brightness when batteries are arranged in different ways in a circuit? In this activity you will explore different arrangements of batteries, see how batteries are arranged in flashlights and portable radios, create dimming switches, and study cell (battery) anatomy.

◆Objective

To create different arrangements of batteries in a circuit and determine how these arrangements influence bulb brightness

To explore arrangements of batteries in common electrical devices and to identify the essential components of a simple cell or battery

◆Procedure

1. **Challenge:** Make a brighter bulb. Use one battery to light a bulb and notice the brightness of the bulb. Now use two batteries to get the bulb to glow more brightly. Draw a picture below showing the arrangement you invented for solving the problem.

2a. There are six circuit arrangements on the next page. Without testing the arrangements first, write an "X" by the arrangements that you predict will cause the bulb to glow more brightly, as compared to a single-battery arrangement.

b.   Now, test each of these circuits and write "B" by those arrangements with a bright bulb, "D" by those with a dim bulb, and "NL" by those that produce no light. Because one arrangement produces a short circuit, do not leave any circuits hooked up for more that 30 seconds.

3.   You have found two circuits that do not light the bulb.

a.   Circuit _____ does not light the bulb because (circle x or y):

  x. Both parts of the bulb are connected to the same ends of the batteries. For electricity to flow, the bulb must be connected to different ends of the batteries.

  y. More electricity travels through a "short circuit" loop than through the bulb loop. A battery in a circuit with another battery (opposite ends connected) can create a short circuit loop.

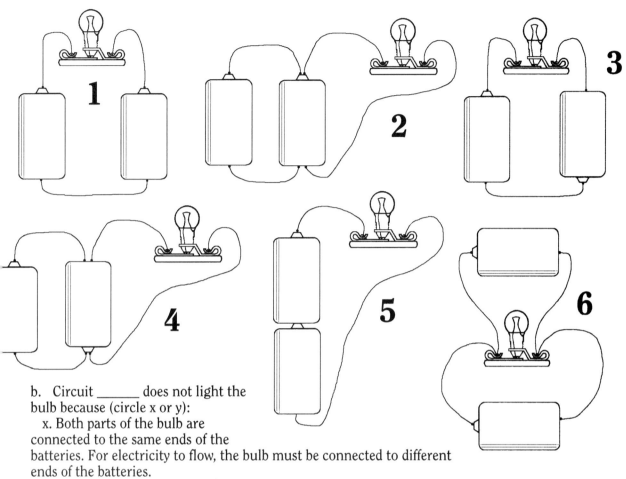

b. Circuit _____ does not light the bulb because (circle x or y):

x. Both parts of the bulb are connected to the same ends of the batteries. For electricity to flow, the bulb must be connected to different ends of the batteries.

y. More electricity travels through a short circuit loop than through the bulb loop. A battery in a circuit with another battery (opposite ends connected) can create a short circuit loop.

c. What is the same about the two circuits in the diagram that produce the *brightly* glowing bulbs? (circle x or y)

x. In the "bulb" circuit or loop, the opposite ends of the batteries are connected either directly or indirectly through wires and the bulb.

y. The same ends of the batteries are connected to each other, even though different ends of the battery or batteries are connected to the bulb.

d. What is the same about the two circuits in the diagram that produce the *dimly* glowing bulbs? (circle x or y)

x. In the "bulb" circuit or loop, the opposite ends of the batteries are connected either directly or indirectly through wires and the bulb.

y. The same ends of the batteries are connected to each other, even though different ends of the battery or batteries are connected to the bulb.

e. There are two circuits that produce *brightly* glowing bulbs. Would you describe the arrangement of batteries in those circuits as series or parallel? _____.

f. There are two circuits that produce *dimly* glowing bulbs. Would you describe the arrangement of batteries in those circuits as series or parallel? _____.

g. If you left a brightly glowing arrangement and a dimly glowing arrangement hooked up for a long time, which one would keep the bulb glowing for the longest period of time?

h. When batteries are hooked up in series (so that the end of each battery is connected to the opposite end of another battery) they cause the bulb to glow (brightly or dimly) _____.

i. When batteries are hooked up in parallel, they cause the bulb to glow (brightly or dimly) _____.

4a. If you have a flashlight or a portable radio or cassette player, open the battery compartment and see how the batteries are arranged. Would you conclude that batteries in these devices are arranged more often in series or in parallel? _____.

In case you do not have a flashlight or portable radio or cassette player available, take a look at the following drawings and determine whether or not the batteries are arranged in series or in parallel.

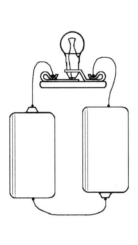 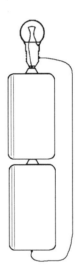 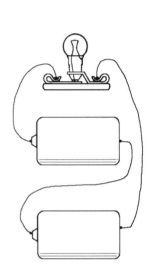

b. The batteries in the above devices are arranged in (series or parallel) _____.

c. The batteries in these devices are arranged to provide (circle x or y):
    x. greater "power" to the device. These arrangements will produce brightly lighted bulbs for shorter periods of time.
    y. less "power" to the device, but over a longer time period. These arrangements will produce dimly lighted bulbs for longer periods of time.

5. To meet the following challenge, you will build a dimming circuit by connecting wires to a bulb, batteries, and paper clip switches. The dimming circuit you will create will *not* operate like the circuits and switches used in your home to dim lights.

You will make two switches from metal paper clips and pieces of thin cardboard. To make a switch, attach two paper clips to the piece of cardboard as shown. Slide a wire under each paper clip. When the paper clips are moved so they touch or overlap, electricity can flow from one wire through both paper clips to the other wire. The switch is closed or "on." When the paper clips are moved so they are not touching, electricity cannot flow from one wire to the other and the switch is open or "off."

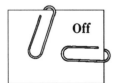 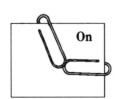

Challenge: Build a dimming circuit. Look at the following arrangement of two batteries, two switches, three wires, and one bulb in its holder.

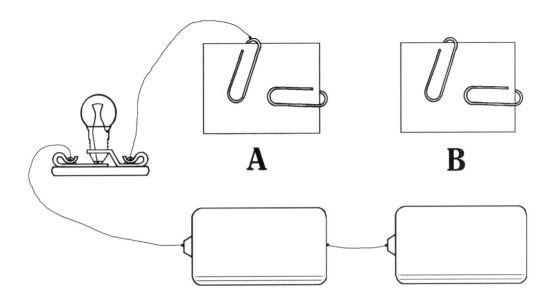

Where would you add three more wires so that all the following conditions are met:
(1) When switch B is on (or closed), the bulb is bright
(2) When switch A is on (closed), the bulb is dim,
(3) When both switches A and B are on (closed), the bulb is dim, and
(4) When both switches A and B are off (open), the bulb is not on.

a.   Use the materials to solve the problem and then draw where three more wires should go in the diagram above.

b.   Use what you know about the arrangements of batteries in a circuit to explain why the bulb is bright when switch B is closed and switch A is open.

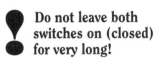

Do not leave both switches on (closed) for very long!

_____

_____

c.   Why is the bulb dim when only switch A is on?

_____

_____

d.   When both switches are on, a short circuit loop is created. Where? Recall that a short circuit loop is an easy pathway and exists where electricity can travel through wires from one end of the battery to the other end without going through a light bulb or other electrical device.

_____

_____

e. When both switches are on, the bulb is dimly lit. This is because (circle x or y):

x. the battery that is in the "short or easy" loop is not helping to produce a flow of electricity through the bulb loop.

y. both batteries are in the "short" loop and work against each other as they try to make the electricity flow in opposite directions through the bulb.

6. Batteries come in different sizes. The common batteries come in "D, C, AA, and AAA" sizes. All of these batteries have the same voltage (1.5 volts) and, unless they are alkaline or rechargeable batteries, are usually made out of the same materials. The larger D battery is made using larger amounts of the same kind of materials used in the C, AA, and the very small AAA battery. Each of these 1.5 volt batteries, if hooked up to a bulb, would produce the same brightness in the bulb. The size of the battery does not necessarily determine bulb brightness. However, the D battery would keep a bulb lighted or a portable radio playing for a longer period of time than the other batteries.

The voltage, not the size, of a battery determines how bright a bulb will glow when hooked up to the battery. If you use the same bulb, more voltage will produce a brighter light. Some batteries have 6 and 9 volts. Bulbs have to be matched to the voltage of the battery. Batteries with higher voltages will burn out (melt the filament in) some bulbs.

There is a relationship between batteries in series, voltage, and bulb brightness. When the voltage increases, bulb brightness increases. You have discovered for yourself that when two batteries are arranged in series (opposite ends of different batteries connected), bulb brightness also increases. If you added a third battery in series, the bulb would become brighter still or burn out. In fact, four 1.5 volt batteries arranged in series would produce the same bulb brightness as one 6 volt battery. One 6 volt battery and two 1.5 volt batteries arranged in series would produce the same bulb brightness as one 9 volt battery.

When batteries are arranged in series (in the proper direction), their voltages are added to determine the voltage for the circuit. If too many batteries are added in series, the bulb in the circuit will "burn out." The

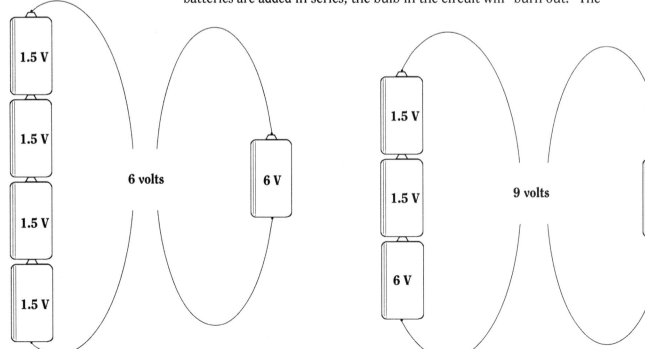

bulb burns or goes out because the filament in the bulb gets too hot, breaks, and creates an open circuit. Bulbs can have different filaments. The filaments in some bulbs are designed to be used in 3-volt circuits. Filaments in other bulbs are designed to be used in 6-volt circuits. A bulb designed for a 6-volt circuit and used in a 3-volt circuit might not glow at all. When you buy bulbs for flash lights (often two 1.5 volt batteries in series producing 3 volts) and battery-powered lanterns (6 volts), make sure that the bulb matches the voltage of the circuit.

When you look at a common flashlight battery you do not see the working parts. What you see are coverings. If you watch your gloved teacher take apart a battery, you will see that with a bit of a struggle and with the danger of being cut by sharp metal, a pair of pliers can be used to peel away the cardboard and/or metal cylindrical side covering of the battery. With the side

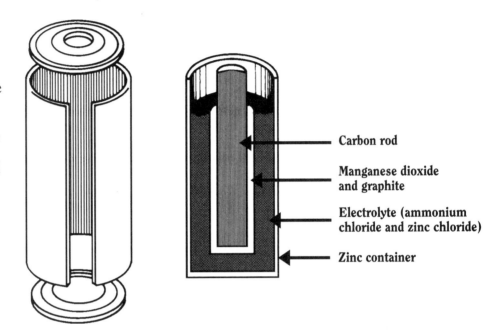

removed, the metal top and bottom cap easily come off. A black rod will stick up a short distance on the top of the battery. The rod is carbon and care should be taken not to break it. The tar from around the carbon rod can be removed and discarded. What is left is the actual working battery. The battery consists of a zinc metal container filled with a black, moist material and in that material is a carbon rod. A battery is simply a bucket of gunk (manganese dioxide, graphite, ammonium chloride, and zinc chloride) with a stick in it.

Carbon rod

Manganese dioxide and graphite

Electrolyte (ammonium chloride and zinc chloride)

Zinc container

This common dry cell produces electricity from chemical reactions among three materials:
• the metal zinc (the outside container)
• an electrolyte—a wet paste of ammonium chloride and zinc chloride (next to the container)
• a paste of manganese dioxide and powdered graphite (in the center of the battery and surrounding the carbon rod).

The carbon rod does not chemically interact; it merely carries or conducts electrons from the outside into the manganese dioxide and powdered graphite.

In one of the first current electricity activities, you discovered that a bulb could be lighted with one battery and only one wire. With all the coverings removed from the battery, WHO NEEDS A WIRE?
If you have an uncovered battery, discover how to light a bulb with just the battery—no wire needed. Draw a picture showing how you solved the problem.

GUIDE TO ACTIVITY 21

The Power Structure and Cell Anatomy

◆What is happening?

In this activity students will discover that when batteries are arranged in series in a circuit (the same ends of the batteries point in the same direction), bulb brightness increases as the number of batteries in the series increases. The students will see that most often batteries are arranged in series in flashlights and portable radios and cassette players. Students will learn that the greater the voltage of a battery, the brighter it will light a given bulb. This leads to the idea that when batteries are arranged in series and the bulb brightens, the voltages of the batteries are added, producing a greater voltage for the circuit.

Students also explore the inside of the common dry cell (not alkaline or rechargeable) and find that it consists of a zinc container, a carbon rod, and some black paste. They discover how to use a naked battery (stripped of the coverings) to light a bulb without the use of a wire.

◆Time management

Two class periods of about 40–60 minutes each should be enough time to complete the activity and discuss the results.

◆Preparation

In addition to gathering the materials and checking the batteries and bulbs, cut two 5 cm X 5 cm pieces of cardboard for each group.

With heavy gloves protecting your hands, use a pair of long-nosed pliers to remove the coverings from 3 or 4 regular C or D dry cells. For each battery, place the coverings (sides, caps, and tar) in one plastic bag and the naked battery in another plastic bag.

❗ Use care when taking apart batteries. Never take apart any battery unless it is a regular AAA, AA, C, or D dry cell. Do not take apart alkaline batteries or rechargeable batteries.

◆Suggestions for further study

If extra bulbs are available, determine how many batteries in series it takes to burn out a #48 bulb. What happens inside the bulb when it "burns out?"

Design an investigation to determine how long the different size batteries (D, C, AA, and AAA) will keep a bulb lighted.

Do some consumer testing to find out if different brands of batteries last longer as claimed in advertisements.

◆Answers

1. A two-battery arrangement that makes the bulb glow brightly is shown at left.

2b. Circuits 3 and 5 will produce a bright bulb and should be labeled with a "B." Circuits 2 and 6 will produce a dim bulb and should be labeled with a "D." Circuits 1 and 4 will not light and should be labeled with an "NL."

3a. Circuit 1 does not light because (x) both parts of the bulb are connected to the same ends of a battery. For electricity to flow, the bulb must be connected to different ends of the battery or batteries.

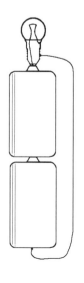

b.   Circuit 4 does not light because (y) the electricity travels more through a "short circuit" loop than through the bulb loop. A battery in a circuit with another battery (opposite ends connected) can create a "short circuit" loop.

c.   The two circuits that produce the brightly glowing bulbs are the same in that (x) in the "bulb" circuit or loop, the opposite ends of the batteries are connected either directly or indirectly through wires and the bulb. To make a complete loop, the electricity must go through each battery and the bulb.

d.   The two circuits that produce dimly glowing bulbs are the same in that (y) the same ends of the batteries are connected to each other, even though different ends of the battery or batteries are connected to the bulb.

e.   The arrangement of batteries in the circuits with *brightly* glowing bulbs would be described as a <u>series</u> arrangement.

f.   The arrangement of batteries in the circuits with *dimly* glowing bulbs would be described as a <u>parallel</u> arrangement.

g.   The dimly glowing arrangement would keep the bulb glowing for the longest period of time.

h.   When batteries are hooked up in series (so that the end of each battery is connected to the opposite end of another battery) they cause the bulb to glow <u>brightly</u>.

i.   When batteries are hooked up in parallel, they cause the bulb to glow <u>dimly</u>.

4a.   Batteries in flashlights and portable radios and cassette players are usually arranged in series.

b.   The batteries in the devices are arranged in <u>series</u>.

c.   The batteries in these devices are arranged to provide (x) greater "power" to the device. These arrangements will produce brightly lighted bulbs for shorter periods of time.

5a.   The arrangement of wires which solves the problem is shown at right.

b.   When switch B is closed and switch A is open, the two batteries are in series and cause the bulb to glow brightly.

c.   When only switch A is on (closed), only one of the batteries is connected to the bulb and the bulb glows dimly.

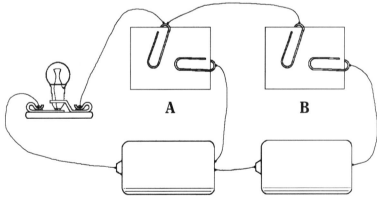

A   **B**

d.   When both switches A and B are closed, the battery that is not connected to the bulb is in a short circuit loop because there is a continuous, easy (no bulbs or motors) path of conductors through the switches and wires from one end of the battery to the other end.

e.   When both switches are on, the bulb is dimly lit. This is because (x) the battery that is in the "short or easy" loop is not helping to produce a flow of electricity through the bulb loop.

6.   The bulb can be lit with a naked battery and no wire as shown. All that is necessary for the bulb to light is that one part of the bulb (thread or bump) touches the carbon rod and the other part of the bulb touches the zinc container at any point.

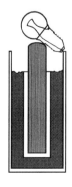

ACTIVITY 22 WORKSHEET

Rolling Tennis Balls and Electrical Current

◆Background

We have talked about electricity flowing through wires and bulbs. What exactly is flowing or moving in the wires? At what rate does it flow? We will use a model to answer these questions. Models look like and sometimes work like real things. Many toys are models. Fashion models are real people but they are not the real "us." They show what we "might" look like if we wear certain clothes or jewelry.

Scientists use and create working models to help them understand things they cannot directly observe. For example, we cannot directly observe atoms, but scientists have created models of atoms which we see illustrated in books. In this activity we will use a rolling tennis ball model to help us understand the electrical concepts of current.

◆Objective

To use a model to understand the concept of electrical current

◆Procedure

1. Look at the diagram of the tennis ball model to see how it will work. Five tennis balls will be rolling at once down the inclined tracks. A sixth ball, the one that rolls off the bottom track, will be lifted from the bottom ramp to the top of the top ramp and released to begin rolling again. The tennis balls will continue to move down the track and be lifted from the bottom to the top track.

Five students will be gatekeepers (GK#1 . . . GK#5). They will stand at certain places along the tracks (see below) and stop each ball as it rolls to them. Each gatekeeper will not allow his or her ball to roll until the next gatekeeper down the track has released his or her ball. Gatekeeper #3 (see below) will have to change the ball from the top track to the bottom track. A sixth student, called the Lifter, will lift to the top track each ball that rolls off the bottom track. No tennis

Materials

For the whole class:

•Two 2.5-meter sections of grooved wooden or metal strips down which tennis balls can be rolled. The top of the top track should be about the height of a chair seat off the floor or working surface. The top of the bottom track should be half the chair seat height off the floor or surface.

•six tennis balls

•one watch or clock that measures seconds

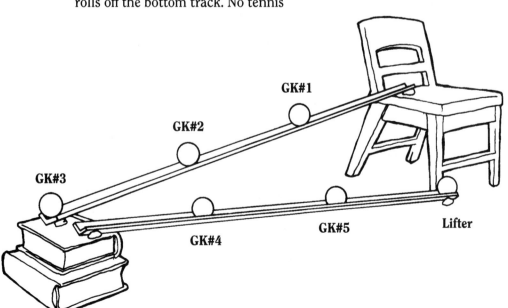

balls will be pushed down the tracks.
REVIEW:
• There are five gatekeepers and one lifter.
• Each gatekeeper (and the lifter) stops the ball that rolls to him or her.
• Each gatekeeper releases a ball only when the next gatekeeper has released his or her tennis ball.
• Tennis balls cannot be pushed down the tracks.
   To start the model working, each gatekeeper and the lifter first holds a ball motionless on the track at their respective positions (see the diagram). Then all the tennis balls are released at the same time when the lifter (now acting as starter) lifts his or her tennis ball from the bottom track to the top track.

2.   In order to get a smooth working model and some consistent data from that model, the gatekeepers and lifter should put in a little practice and develop a rhythm. They should reach a skill level where they can get the tennis balls to make at least two round trips without mistakes.
   At what rate are the tennis balls moving when the model is working? There are different ways of answering this question. We will, however, answer the question by counting the number of tennis balls that pass a particular point each second.
• Each person observing the model picks a specific point along the track. The points can be different for different people.
• When the model is working smoothly, have a time keeper say "Start" and then say "Stop" after 20 seconds have passed.
• During the 20 seconds, each person counts the number of tennis balls which pass their chosen point.

a.   Record the number of tennis balls passing your point in 20 seconds

_____.

• Calculate tennis ball travel rate:
Tennis ball travel rate = number of tennis balls/20 seconds
Divide the number of tennis balls counted by 20 seconds to get the number of tennis balls passing each second.

b.   Your tennis ball travel rate is _____ tennis balls passing each second.
• Check with other students to see how the travel rates at different points compared.

c.   What general statement might you make about travel rate along the track?

_____

_____

3.   How are the parts of the model like an electric circuit? The tennis balls represent current that moves in the wires of an electrical circuit. The ramps represent wires. The person who moves the tennis balls from the bottom ramp to the top ramp represents the battery in a real circuit.

4.   What does tennis ball travel rate have to do with what happens when electricity moves through wires? Obviously, tennis balls are not moving in the wires. Wires, like all matter, are made of atoms which are made of protons, electrons, and neutrons. The protons (+ charge) and neutrons (no charge) make up the nucleus or center of each atom. Orbiting around the outside of the nucleus are the electrons (– charge).
   In solid metals (like wires), the nuclei jiggle around but do not move easily from one place to another. Also, in solid metals some electrons are

not held tightly by their nuclei and can be easily moved from one atom to another. In fact, some electrons are so loosely held to the nucleus that they are considered free. There is one free electron for each copper atom in a copper wire.

What moves in a wire carrying electricity are electrons (negative charges).

5.   What do the tennis balls represent? Because electrons move in wires and tennis balls move in the model, you might think that a tennis ball would refer to an electron. Instead, each tennis ball represents a very large number of electrons, in fact 6.25 million-million-million electrons (negative charges). Together that many charges make up a unit of charge called a coulomb. Each tennis ball represents a coulomb.

Why don't we count electrons instead of coulombs? The charge of one electron is so small and the electrons are so numerous that it makes more sense to measure the charge in terms of a large number of electrons.

6.   What does tennis ball travel rate represent? Each tennis ball refers to a coulomb of charge. Tennis ball travel rate is the number of tennis balls passing a point in a second.

The tennis ball travel rate represents the number of coulombs passing a certain point in the wire each second.

In electrical terms, this travel rate or flow rate is called current. The more coulombs that pass a point in a second, the greater the electrical current. Electrical current or flow rate is measured in amperes. One ampere is the flow rate of one coulomb of charge passing a point in a second.

We have described electrons moving in wires from the negative end of the battery to the positive end. This direction of flow is correct in that electrons, being negatively charged, will move away from the negative end of the battery and toward the positive end. Later on in your study of physics you will learn that current is defined by convention to be in terms of coulombs per second and in the direction of *positive* charge flow. The conventional way of describing current direction (positive charges moving from positive to negative) is opposite to what we have described (negatively charged electrons moving from negative to positive). Because the convention asks us to think in terms of positive movement when in fact negative charges move in the wires of our circuits, we will set aside the convention for the time being and think of current as the rate of electron (negative charge) flow. You will discover later how the conventional definition of current makes it easier to think about currents in more complicated circuits and in situations where positive charges are moving.

When one coulomb passes a point in a second we say that the current is 1 ampere or 1 amp. If 2 coulombs pass a point in a second, the current is 2 amperes or 2 amps.

The current in the wires running through a 100 watt light bulb in your home is about 1 ampere. This means that there is about 1 coulomb of charge entering (and leaving) the filament of the bulb each second. This means that there are about 6.25 million-million-million electrons entering and leaving the filament each second.

a.   The tennis ball travel rate you found earlier (step 2b) was
_____ per second. What is that flow rate in terms of amperes?
_____. Recall that a tennis ball represents a coulomb of charge and that an ampere is one coulomb per second.

GUIDE TO ACTIVITY 22

Rolling Tennis Balls and Electrical Current

◆What is happening

Students observe a working model of an electrical circuit. They record the rate at which charges (tennis balls) move through the circuit. Students learn that the rate of electrical flow (current) is described in terms of the number of coulombs passing a point in the circuit each second. The rate of one coulomb passing each second is defined as an ampere. The model and the definition of current are used in the next few activities.

◆Time management

Two class periods of 40–60 minutes each should be enough time to complete the activity and discuss the student responses.

◆Preparation

The 2.5-meter ramps can be strips of molding. To keep the molding from sagging under its own weight, it might be necessary to glue strips of wood to the bottom of the molding. You can also use pieces of reasonably inexpensive plastic gutter for the ramps. The only drawback of gutter is that some students won't be able to see the tennis balls rolling down the gutters. You could make your own ramps by nailing thin strips of molding to a wider base to form a channel for the tennis balls to roll down.

◆Suggestions for further study

What are various things that might be done to increase or decrease the current observed in the model? Try some of these things.

Suppose someone says that the battery makes electrons and the electrons are used up as they go through the circuit. Is this statement supported by the model? If so, how? If not, why not?

◆Answers

2a and b.   Answers will vary depending on the model and the students working the model.

c.   Students might predict that the rates of travel will be greater on the lower ramp or that the rate of travel will be lesser on the upper ramp. However, students should find that the rate of travel is nearly the same at all places along the ramp.

6a. Answers will vary depending on the model and the students working the model.

ACTIVITY 23 WORKSHEET

Volts: The "Kick" in the Current

◆Background

Batteries are often identified by the number of volts they provide. Batteries such as C, D, and AA provide 1.5 volts. Many car batteries provide 12 volts. Household electricity provides 120 volts. So, what is a volt? In this activity, you will find that as voltage increases, current increases, all else being the same. You will also learn that voltage is the amount of energy given to each coulomb of charge by the battery or power source.

◆Objective

To use the tennis ball model to learn about the concept of volt and to see how voltage is related to current

◆Procedure

1. Set up the ramps for the model so that both ramps have the same slant but in opposite directions. The top of the top ramp should be about 45 to 50 cm above the bottom of the bottom ramp.

    A group of students should get the tennis ball model working as in Activity 22. While the model is running smoothly, determine the current in terms of coulombs/second (amperes). To do this, start by counting the number of tennis balls (coulombs) passing a certain point in 20 seconds.

a. How many tennis balls pass a point in 20 seconds? _____.

b. The number of tennis balls passing the point in one second is

    _____.

c. The current in amperes is _____.

2a. Predict: If the ramps are made steeper (the top and bottom of the ramps are moved farther apart), will the current increase or decrease?_____

    Now make the ramps steeper so that the top of the top ramp is about a meter above the bottom of the bottom ramp. Both ramps should have the same slant but in opposite directions.

    A group of students should get the tennis ball model working. As in Activity 22, while the model is running smoothly, determine the current in amperes. To do this, start by counting the number of tennis balls (coulombs) passing a certain point in 20 seconds.

b. How many tennis balls pass a point in 20 seconds?

    _____.

Materials

For the whole class:

•the two 2.5 meter ramps and six tennis balls used in the tennis ball model in Activity 22.

•a slider which is made from a 10 cm X 46 cm piece of manila folder. The piece of manila folder is folded to form a "V" with 10 cm X 23 cm sides. This is simply a 10 cm section cut from the end of a manila folder. A tennis ball will roll into the slider and slide it until both stop.

•a meter stick

For each group:

•two batteries in their battery holders.

•one #48 bulb

•three wires

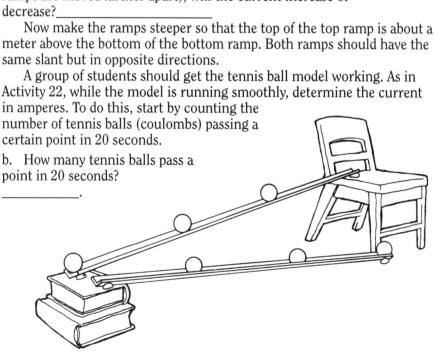

c.   The number of tennis balls passing the point in one second is
_____.

d.   The current in amperes is _____.

e.   When the ramps are steeper (there is a greater vertical distance between the ends of the ramps), is the current greater or lesser than before? _____

f.   When the ramps are steeper, the lifter has to do (more work or less work) _____ in lifting each tennis ball from the bottom to the top ramp.

g.   The lifter would run out of energy (more quickly or less quickly) _____ if the ramp was steeper.

3.   To see how this model is like real electricity, we have to go back to batteries and bulbs.
Challenge: Using one bulb in a bulb holder, two batteries in holders, and three wires, construct two different circuits (not at the same time). One circuit should have a larger current than the other. In one circuit the bulb should be brighter than in the other circuit. You may not need all of the materials in each circuit.

a.   Draw the electrical circuit that you think has the greater current.

b.   Draw the electrical circuit that you think has the lesser current.

c.   Which of the above two circuits is most like the model with the steeper ramps? _____
      Each battery has 1.5 volts written on it. When batteries are hooked up in series (the positive (bump) end of one battery hooked up to the negative (flat) end of the other battery), the volts add up. Two batteries connected in series produce 1.5 + 1.5 = 3 volts. So when there are 3 volts instead of 1.5 (all else being the same), there is greater current, more energy, and a single bulb in the circuit glows brighter.
      Having 3 volts is like having steeper ramps. Having 1.5 volts is like having less steep ramps.

4.   Set up a single section of ramp, 2.5 m long, so that the top end is about 25 cm off a flat surface (floor or table top). A cardboard "V" slider will be placed at the bottom of the ramp and will catch the ball when the ball rolls into it from the top of the ramp. The slider, with the ball pushing it, will slide along and come to a stop a certain distance from the end of the ramp. Observe this and record the distance the ball pushes the slider after rolling from the top of the ramp.

a.   With the top of the ramp about 25 cm off the floor, how far does the ball push the slider? _____.

Now raise the top of the ramp about 50 cm off the floor. Observe the ball roll down the ramp and into the slider.

b.   With the top of the ramp about 50 cm off the floor, how far does the ball push the slider? _____.

c.   When the ball starts to roll from a point higher off the floor, the ball moves the slider a (greater or lesser)_____distance.

d.   When the ball is released from a point higher off the floor, the ball has (more or less)_____energy at the bottom of the ramp, compared to the point lower to the floor.

Energy is the *ability* to do work—to push or pull things over a distance. It is important to note that an object does not have to be doing anything to another object to have energy. An object with energy must at least have the *ability* to push or pull other objects over a distance.

e.   Does a ball held motionless at the top of a ramp have the ability to push objects through a distance? _____ How do you know?

_____

_____

f.   A ball has more energy at the top of a ramp that is (lower or higher)_____ off the floor.

When the ball is raised from the table top and placed at the top end of the ramp, it is given energy (the ability to push or pull through a distance). The ball gets that energy from the person lifting it. The higher the person lifts the ball, the more energy is transferred from the person to the ball, the more energy the ball has as it rolls down the ramp, and the more energy the ball can transfer to the slider.

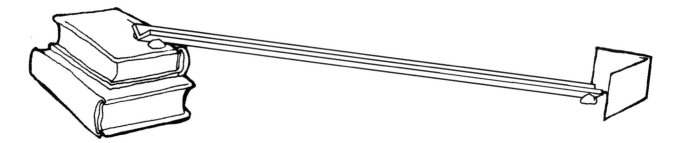

In an electrical circuit, the battery is like the person who lifts the tennis balls to the top end of the ramp. The battery provides energy to the electrons or coulombs (tennis balls). Energy is measured in joules. If a battery gives each coulomb of charge one joule of energy, the battery is supplying the circuit with one volt. If the battery supplies three joules of energy to each coulomb (tennis ball) leaving the battery, the battery is supplying three volts to the circuit. The number of volts is the number of joules of energy given to each coulomb of charge (tennis ball).

When two batteries are arranged in series, the voltages from the batteries are added. This is similar to having a greater distance between the top and bottom of the ramps in the model. The greater the distance, the more energy the tennis balls have. The greater the voltage, the greater the energy each coulomb of charge has. With a single 1.5 volt battery, each coulomb gets 1.5 joules of energy. With 3 volts (two 1.5 volt batteries arranged in series) each coulomb of charge gets 3 joules of energy. All else being equal, the more voltage, the greater amount of energy provided to each coulomb. Greater voltage results in greater current and brighter bulbs.

GUIDE TO ACTIVITY 23

Volts: The "Kick" in the Current

◆What is happening?

Students observe the tennis ball model working and see that the current increases when the ramp heights are greater. Students also learn that when a tennis ball is placed higher on a ramp, the ball has more energy. The energy and current associated with the model are related to volts and current in real circuits. Greater ramp heights are associated with greater voltage. Ramp height (voltage) determines the amount of energy given to the tennis balls (coulombs). In real circuits, greater voltage means that greater energy is given to each coulomb leaving the battery and that electrical current increases.

◆Time management

Two class periods of about 40–60 minutes each should be enough time to complete the activity and discuss the results.

◆Preparation

Cut the V-shaped slider from a manila folder. Set up the tennis ball model.

◆Suggestions for further study

Make a graph of the relationship between how far the ball slides the slider and the vertical height the ball has when it starts to roll down the ramp. Use one ramp and always place the tennis ball at the end of the ramp so the ball always rolls the same distance along the ramp. Elevate the end of the ramp different distances off the flat surface.

When two batteries are hooked up in parallel and are attached to one bulb, the bulb will not glow brighter but will glow for a very long time before the batteries wear out. The batteries do not increase the voltage, but the batteries must share in providing energy to the coulombs. How would you change the tennis ball model so that it would behave like a circuit with two batteries connected in parallel? How would adding a person to the model solve the problem? Where would the person be added?

◆Answers

1a, b, and c.   The answers will vary depending on the model and the students working it.

2a. If the ramps are made steeper (the top and bottom of the ramps are moved farther apart), the current will <u>increase</u>.

b and c.   The number of tennis balls passing per 20 seconds and per one second will vary but will be greater than in step 1 above.

d.   The same will be true of the number of amperes.

e.   When the ramps are steeper (there is a greater vertical distance between the ends of the ramps), the current is <u>greater</u> than before.

f.   When the ramps are steeper, the lifter has to do <u>more work</u> in lifting the tennis balls from the bottom to the top ramp.

g.   The lifter would run out of energy <u>more quickly</u> if the ramp was steeper.

3a. The circuit with the greater current should look like:

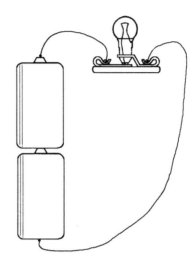

b. The circuit with the lesser current should look like:

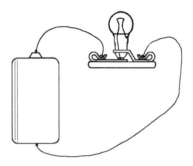

c. The circuit with the greater current (3a) is most like the model with the steeper ramps.

4a and b.   Answers will vary, but the value for the 50-cm-high ramp should be greater than the value for the 25-cm-high ramp.

c. When the ball starts to roll from a point higher off the floor, the ball moves the slider a <u>greater</u> distance.

d. When the ball starts to roll from a point higher off the floor, the ball has <u>more</u> energy at the bottom of the ramp, compared to the point lower to the floor.

e. The ball held motionless at the top of a ramp has energy. If the ball was held motionless on a flat surface and released, it would do nothing. If the ball was held motionless at the top of a ramp and then released, it would start to roll down the ramp and it could do some pushing. The motionless ball at the top of the ramp has something that the motionless ball of the flat surface does not—energy, the ability to do something.

f. A ball has more energy at the top of a higher ramp.

ACTIVITY 24 WORKSHEET

Socking in Resistance and Summarizing With Ohm's Law

◆Background

The previous activity showed that electrical current increases if voltage increases (all else being the same). In this activity, we consider electrical resistance as another factor which influences the current. As electrons move through wires in a closed circuit they encounter resistance to their flow. The amount of resistance will determine (along with voltage) the rate at which the electrons flow or, in other words, the current in the wires. Ohm's law will summarize the relationship among current, voltage, and resistance.

◆Objective

To use the tennis ball model to understand the concept of electrical resistance and to see how the relationship among current, voltage, and resistance is summarized in Ohm's law

◆Procedure

1. Get the tennis ball model working with a group of students. As in Activity 22, while the model is running smoothly, determine the current in amperes. To do this count the number of tennis balls (coulombs) passing a certain point in 20 seconds.

a. _____ tennis balls pass a point in 20 seconds.

b. The number of tennis balls passing the point in one second is

_____.

c. The current in amperes is _____.

2. In Activity 23, you learned that when the slope of the ramps was steeper, the "current" was greater (a greater number of tennis balls passing a point each second—a greater amperage). This greater height of the top of the ramp corresponded to greater voltage in real electrical circuits and resulted in each coulomb of charge receiving more energy (more joules) and traveling faster along the conductor (more amperes). All else being equal, greater voltage produces greater current or amperage.

The same people who worked the model in step 1 above will work the model again. This time, however, one of the gatekeepers will take each tennis ball that comes to him or her and squeeze it through a toeless sock before allowing the ball to roll to the next gatekeeper. After squeezing the ball through the sock, the gatekeeper must place each ball back on the ramp at the point where the ball was taken. The tennis balls must not be pushed down the ramp by any gatekeeper.

When one sock is in the circuit and the model is working, determine the current by counting the number of tennis balls passing a point in 20 seconds.

a. _____ tennis balls pass a point in 20 seconds.

b. The number of tennis balls passing the point in one second is

_____.

c. The current in amperes is _____.

Materials

For the whole class:

•one tennis ball model including 6 tennis balls and two ramps set up like the model in Activity 22

•two old socks, each with the toe end cut off

For each group:

•one battery in a battery holder

•three wires with the ends stripped of insulation

•two #48 bulbs in bulb holders

d. How does the current with the sock in the circuit compare to the current without the sock?

_____

_____

e. When the sock was in the circuit, was the current less only at the sock or at all points along the circuit? _____

3. Next, the team will work the model again, but this time the gatekeeper will have to pass the tennis ball through two toeless socks before allowing the ball to roll to the next gatekeeper. It is important to have one gatekeeper send each ball through two socks.

When two socks are in the circuit and the model is working, determine the current by counting the number of tennis balls passing a point in 20 seconds.

a. _____ tennis balls pass a point in 20 seconds.

b. The number of tennis balls passing the point in one second is

_____.

c. The current in amperes is _____.

d. How does the current with two socks in the circuit compare to the current with one sock in the circuit?

_____

_____

4. **Challenge:** Using two bulbs in bulb holders, one battery in its holder, and three wires, construct two circuits (not at the same time) which you think would be like the one sock and two sock models above. You may not need all of the materials in each circuit. Hint: One circuit should have a bulb glowing with an average brightness and the other circuit should have two bulbs which are dimly lighted.

a. Draw the electrical circuit which is most like the one sock model.

b. Draw the electrical circuit which is most like the two sock model.

c. In which of the above two electrical circuits (the circuit like the two sock or the one sock model) do you believe the current is the least?_____

5. We can look at the model to help us understand the concept of resistance. When the model is run without a sock, the current is relatively large. When a single sock is used in the model, the "current" becomes less. When two socks are used, the current is reduced even more. Similarly, if a wire connects both ends of a battery and creates a short circuit, the wire heats up and the battery quickly "dies" indicating that the current is rather large in the short circuit. When one bulb is placed in a circuit, the bulb glows, the connecting wires do not get hot, and the battery "lives" a reasonable life. When two bulbs are connected in series, both bulbs dimly glow. If a third bulb is added in series, the bulbs may not glow at all and there is little obvious indication of a current.

There is a tendency to think that the rate of electron flow is reduced only in the bulbs where most of the resistance is provided. The model did not show this to be true. When the sock was in the circuit, the current was reduced at all points in the circuit. This is true in electrical circuits as well. In a series circuit, resistance at one point influences current at all points.

Electrical resistance is measured in ohms. If the voltage is one volt and the current or amperage is one ampere, then the resistance is one ohm.

6. Different materials of the same size and shape offer different amounts of resistance to the flow of electricity. Copper, aluminum, and silver offer very little resistance and are good conductors of electricity. Other materials such as plastic, wood, and glass offer much resistance to the flow of electricity and are very poor conductors of electricity.

Long wires provide greater resistance than short wires made of the same material. Thin wires provide greater resistance than thick wires made of the same material.

When materials heat up they usually provide greater resistance to the flow of electricity. When they cool down, resistance goes down. A Dutch scientist named Heike Kamerlingh-Onnes discovered that when he cooled a ring of mercury down (to 269 degrees Celsius below the freezing point of water) and produced a current in the ring, the current continued for many years without any power supply. The cold ring of mercury provided no resistance to the flow of electricity so the flow continued without lessening.

Materials which show no electrical resistance at extremely cold temperatures are called superconductors. Some of the common superconducting materials are aluminum, lead, and tin. Interestingly enough, copper and silver, which are great conductors at room temperatures, do not become superconductors when cooled down.

7. The unit of measure of resistance (ohm) is named after Georg Ohm, a German physicist. In 1826, Georg Ohm summarized the relationship among voltage, current, and resistance with what came to be known as Ohm's law.

Ohm's Law is

$$\text{Current} = \frac{\text{Voltage}}{\text{Resistance}} \qquad \text{or} \qquad \text{Amperes} = \frac{\text{Volts}}{\text{Ohms}}$$

Often, current is labeled "I", voltage is labeled "V" and resistance is labeled "R." Ohm's law expressed in these labels is shown in the following formula:

$$I = \frac{V}{R}$$

In other words, as resistance goes up (more bulbs in series), the current goes down, provided the voltage remains the same. As voltage increases (more batteries in series), the current increases, provided the resistance remains the same.

This formula is saying what you have already learned. If the voltage stays at, let's say 6 volts, and the resistance increases from 1 to 3 to 6 ohms, the current goes from 6 amperes to 2 amperes, to 1 ampere.

Current decreases (6, 2, 1 amperes) when voltage stays constant (6 volts) and the resistance increases (1, 3, 6 ohms):

$$I = \frac{V}{R}$$

$$I = \frac{6 \text{ volts}}{1 \text{ ohm}} = 6 \text{ amperes}$$

$$I = \frac{6 \text{ volts}}{3 \text{ ohms}} = 2 \text{ amperes}$$

$$I = \frac{6 \text{ volts}}{6 \text{ ohms}} = 1 \text{ ampere}$$

If the resistance stays the same, let's say 2 ohms, and the voltage increases from 2 volts to 4 volts to 6 volts, the current goes from 1 ampere to 2 amperes to 3 amperes.

Current increases (1, 2, 3 amperes) when the resistance stays constant (2 ohms) and the voltage increases (2, 4, 6 volts):

$$I = \frac{V}{R}$$

$$I = \frac{2 \text{ volts}}{2 \text{ ohms}} = 1 \text{ ampere}$$

$$I = \frac{4 \text{ volts}}{2 \text{ ohms}} = 2 \text{ amperes}$$

$$I = \frac{6 \text{ volts}}{2 \text{ ohms}} = 3 \text{ amperes}$$

8. Solve the following problems:

Problem 1. A 60-watt light bulb has a resistance of 240 ohms. The voltage in household electricity is 120 volts. Use Ohm's Law to calculate the current going through a 60 watt light bulb.

$$I = \frac{V}{R} \qquad I = \frac{\underline{\quad} \text{ volts}}{\underline{\quad} \text{ ohms}} = \underline{\quad} \text{ amperes}$$

Problem 2. A 1200-watt hair dryer has a resistance of 12 ohms (less than the light bulb). The voltage in household electricity is 120 volts. Use Ohm's Law to calculate the current going through the hair dryer.

$$I = \frac{V}{R} \qquad I = \frac{\underline{\quad} \text{ volts}}{\underline{\quad} \text{ ohms}} = \underline{\quad} \text{ amperes}$$

Notice that in going from problem 1 to problem 2, the resistance decreased, from 240 ohms to 12 ohms, the voltage stayed the same (120 volts), and the current increased. When you decrease the resistance while keeping the voltage the same, the current increases. The opposite is also true—when you increase the resistance while keeping the voltage the same, the current decreases.

Problem 3. A 480-watt stereo system has a resistance of 30 ohms. The voltage in household electricity is 120 volts. Use Ohm's Law to calculate the current going through the stereo.

$$I = \frac{V}{R} \qquad I = \frac{\underline{\quad} \text{ volts}}{\underline{\quad} \text{ ohms}} = \underline{\quad} \text{ amperes}$$

Problem 4. Assume that the electrical company has problems and cannot get 120 volt electricity to your house. Instead, you get 60 volt electricity. Now use Ohm's Law to calculate the current going through your stereo system.

$$I = \frac{V}{R} \qquad I = \frac{\underline{\quad} \text{ volts}}{\underline{\quad} \text{ ohms}} = \underline{\quad} \text{ amperes}$$

Notice that in going from problem 3 to problem 4, the voltage went down, from 120 volts to 60 volts, the resistance stayed the same (30 ohms), and the current decreased.

GUIDE TO ACTIVITY 24

Socking in Resistance and Summarizing with Ohm's Law

◆What is happening?

In this activity, students consider electrical resistance as another factor that influences the current. The tennis ball model will be used as before, but this time one gatekeeper will have to pass each ball through a toeless sock before allowing the ball to roll to the next gatekeeper. The sock will reduce the current and will simulate electrical resistance—particularly the resistance provided by a bulb. In the previous activity, students observed how voltage influenced current. In this activity students will see how resistance influences current. The influence of both voltage and resistance on current will be summarized with Ohm's law.

◆Time management

Two class periods of about 40–60 minutes each should be enough time to complete the activity and discuss the results.

◆Preparation

Set up the ramps for the tennis ball model. Make the slopes rather steep so the current is rather large. Cut the toe ends off two old socks.

◆Suggestions for further study

When you algebraically solve Ohm's law equation for R, you get:

$$R = \frac{V}{I}$$

If you know the voltage and the current for a circuit, you can use this formula to calculate the resistance. Assume that the voltage for the tennis ball model is one volt for each centimeter measured from the bottom end of the bottom ramp to the top end of the top ramp. Figure out the voltage for the model. See step #1 above for the current you calculated. Use the voltage, the current, and the above formula to calculate the resistance for the tennis ball model (no socks).

Use the same voltage, the current you calculated for the one-sock model (see step #2), and the above formula to calculate the resistance for the one-sock tennis ball model.

A 1.5 volt battery is hooked up to a #48 bulb. An instrument for measuring current, called an ammeter, shows that the current in the circuit is about .05 amperes. How much resistance does a #48 bulb provide?

Two 1.5 volt batteries are hooked up in series and these are connected to a circuit in which two #48 bulbs are arranged in series. Use Ohm's law, the information given above, and the resistance you calculated in the last problem to calculate the current for the circuit.

◆Answers

1. The answers for this section will vary depending on the model and the students working the model.

2 and 3.The answers for this section will also vary. One sock, however, should reduce the current substantially, at all points along the circuit. Two socks should reduce the current even more.

4a. The real electrical circuit which is most like the one sock model might be drawn as:

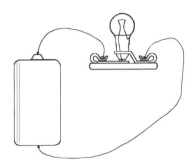

b. The real electrical circuit which is most like the two sock model might be drawn as:

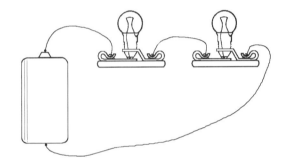

c. The current in the two-bulb circuit will be smaller.

8. Problem 1:

$$I = \frac{V}{R} = \frac{120 \text{ volts}}{240 \text{ ohms}} = 0.5 \text{ amperes}$$

Problem 2:

$$I = \frac{V}{R} = \frac{120 \text{ volts}}{12 \text{ ohms}} = 10 \text{ amperes}$$

Problem 3:

$$I = \frac{V}{R} = \frac{120 \text{ volts}}{30 \text{ ohms}} = 4 \text{ amperes}$$

Problem 4:

$$I = \frac{V}{R} = \frac{60 \text{ volts}}{30 \text{ ohms}} = 2 \text{ amperes}$$

ACTIVITY 25 WORKSHEET

What's a Watt?

◆Background

The electrical term "watt" is widely used. There are 25, 40, 60, and 100 watt light bulbs. The electric space heater has a switch which reads 750 and 1500 watts. Your microwave oven might be rated for 1250 watts. A blow drier for hair might be rated at 1000 watts. When the electrical bill arrives, the charge is based on the how many watts (or kilowatts) have been used in the home during the billing period. With all the "watts" around, the question arises, "What's a watt?"

◆Objective

To use the tennis ball model to arrive at an understanding of the concept of a watt

◆Procedure

1. Recall that a volt is the amount of energy given to each coulomb of charge by the battery. For each volt, each coulomb of charge receives one joule of energy. If a battery supplies six volts, then each coulomb of charge receives 6 joules of energy. If a battery supplies 1.5 volts, then each coulomb of charge receives 1.5 joules of energy. This means that each coulomb which leaves the negative end of the battery has a certain amount of energy (the number of joules equal to the volts) which it can give up in traveling along the circuit to the positive end of the battery.

2. How much energy passes into the conductors of the tennis ball model circuit each second? Recall that a tennis ball represents a coulomb of charge (a bunch of electrons numbering 6.25 million-million-million). Each tennis ball is given an amount of energy (in joules) which is equal to the voltage supplied by the battery. Let's assume that the battery in the model is a 2 volt battery. This means that each coulomb leaving the battery would have 2 joules of energy.

Challenge: With a working tennis ball model, how would you determine the amount of energy (in terms of joules, not coulombs) entering the circuit from the battery each second?

Some hints for meeting the challenge: You cannot observe this directly because energy is not an object and cannot be observed. You can observe the number of tennis balls entering the circuit from the battery each second. Try counting the number of tennis balls (coulombs) entering the circuit (top ramp) in 20 seconds.

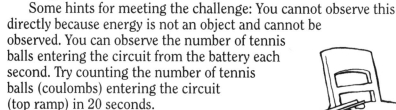

Materials

For the whole class:
•6 tennis balls and two ramps set up as described in Activity 22

From there you can figure out the number of coulombs entering each second and from there you can figure out how much energy is entering the circuit each second.

Observe a working tennis ball model and determine the amount of energy entering a circuit each second.

a. The number of tennis balls (coulombs) entering the circuit in a 20 second period is_____.

b. The number of tennis balls (coulombs) entering the circuit each second would be_____.

Because the voltage is assumed to be 2 volts, each coulomb would receive 2 joules of energy from the battery.

c. The number of joules (energy) entering the wires each second would be _____.

To arrive at an answer for "c" above, you likely multiplied the number of coulombs entering each second (this is current or amperage) and the number of joules given each coulomb by the battery (this is voltage). If, for example, there are two coulombs entering per second (two amperes of current) and each coulomb enters with 2 joules of energy (2 volts), then the amount of energy entering the circuit each second is 4 joules (2 coulombs per second × 2 volts for each coulomb).

Multiply the current (amperes or coulombs per second) and voltage (volts or joules for each coulomb) to get the amount of energy transferred from the battery to the coulombs each second.

The rate of energy transfer (how fast and how much energy is transferred) is known as electrical power.

Power = Current × Voltage

Power is the rate of energy transfer. Something powerful can transfer a lot of energy quickly. Power is measured in watts.

One watt is one joule of energy being transferred per second. One watt of power exists when one ampere of current is produced by one volt.

Power = current × voltage = energy transferred per second (number of joules per second)

Watts= amperes × volts

$$\text{Watts} = \left(\frac{\text{coulombs}}{\text{second}}\right) \times \left(\frac{\text{joules}}{\text{coulomb}}\right) = \left(\frac{\text{joules}}{\text{second}}\right)$$

d. In "c" above you calculated the amount of energy transferred per second into the wires from the battery. What is this rate of energy transfer in terms of watts? _____.

3. Many appliances, such as light bulbs, hair driers, microwave ovens, electric heaters, air conditioners, and stereos are labeled with the number of watts they use. For example, a light bulb may be labeled as a 100-watt light bulb. The "100 watts" refers to the amount of energy transferred to the bulb per second. Recall that a watt is one joule of energy per second. A 100-watt light bulb receives 100 joules of energy per second. A 60-watt light bulb receives 60 joules of energy per second. The 100-watt bulb receives more energy per second than the 60-watt bulb and consequently can give off more energy in the form of heat and light. A 50-watt stereo system receives 50 joules of energy per second. A 100-watt stereo system receives 100 joules of energy per second. The 100-watt system can produce a greater amount of sound energy (volume) per second than can the 50-watt system.

a. You might find some interest in going on a watt hunt in your home. Which do you think uses more energy, in watts—your toaster, hair drier, television, or refrigerator?

_____

_____

b. A television did not indicate the wattage, but did indicate that it used 1.5 amperes when connected to 120-volt household electricity. What is the wattage of this television? _____

4. The number of watts indicates how many joules of energy are used per second. A 75 watt stereo system can receive 75 joules of energy per second. If you turn the system on for 60 seconds, the system will receive a total of 4500 joules of energy during those 60 seconds.
Total energy received or transferred = watts × time
Total energy = 75 watts × 60 seconds = 4500 watt-seconds

$$\text{Total energy} = 75 \left(\frac{\text{joules}}{\text{second}}\right) \times 60 \text{ seconds} = 4500 \text{ joules}$$

Notice that a watt-second is the same thing as a joule and that both are measures of energy.

The longer an appliance is on and working, the more total energy the appliance receives and the more energy it gives out in the form of heat or light or sound.

When we pay our electrical bills, we pay for the total amount of energy used during a time period. If we measured the total number of watt-seconds (joules) used in a home during a two month period, we would end up with a very large number. Even a 75-watt stereo turned on for one minute uses 4500 joules. To get numbers of a reasonable size, electrical companies use kilowatts (kW) and hours (H) rather than watts and seconds. One kilowatt is 1000 watts or 1000 joules of energy used per second. The total energy used in a time period is measured in kilowatt-hours (kWh). A kilowatt-hour (kWh) is the amount of energy used by an appliance rated at 1 kilowatt (hair drier or space heater) running for one hour of time.

The electrical company measures how many kilowatt-hours are used by your home during a two month period. They figure how much money you owe them by multiplying the total number of kilowatt-hours used and the charge for each kilowatt-hour. For example, for a two month period the bill might show that 1350 KWHs (kilowatt-hours) of energy were used. At a charge of 8.75 cents for each kilo-watt hour, the amount of money due would be:
1350 kWh × 8.75 cents for each kWh = 11812.50 cents
or $118.13

You can figure out how much it costs you to run your TV or stereo for an evening (5 hours). For example, assume your TV is rated at 200 watts. The 200 watts can be changed into kilowatts by dividing by 1000. With 0.2 kilowatts running for 5 hours, the total energy used would be 1 kilowatt-hour (0.2 kW × 5 h = 1 kWh). At a cost of 8.75 cents for each kWh, one night of TV costs 8.75 cents. Not a bad deal—less than a dime for one night of entertainment.

GUIDE TO ACTIVITY 25

What's a Watt?

◆What is happening?

Students learn about the concept of a watt from observing the tennis ball model. They know that voltage refers to the amount of energy given to each coulomb of charge by the battery. They know that current is the number of coulombs passing into (and out of) the wires each second. From these two ideas and from observations of a working tennis ball model, students calculate the amount of energy carried into the wires each second. The amount of energy being transferred each second is defined as electrical power and a watt is defined as one joule of energy being transferred per second.

From these basic definitions and from knowledge about the watts attributed to various household appliances, the total amounts of energy (watt-seconds or joules) used by those appliances over certain time periods are calculated. Students also learn that a kilowatt-hour is an energy unit used by power companies and they see how kilowatt-hours and cost for each kilowatt-hour are used to calculate the electrical bill received from the power company.

◆Time management

Two class periods of 40–60 minutes each should be enough time to complete the activity and discuss the results.

◆Preparation

The two ramps used for the tennis ball model should be set up as shown in Activity 22.

◆Suggestions for further study

How could you *hear* the power of a lighted 100-watt light bulb? Does anyone you know own a 100-watt stereo system? Why might the stereo not provide an accurate demonstration of the power of the lighted bulb?

Find the electrical meter for your school. Take a reading at the beginning of the day and at the end of the day. Read the dials from left to right and write down each number in order. When the hand of the dial is between numbers (and most will be) write down the lower number. Subtract the reading at the beginning of the day from the reading at the end of the day to get the number of kilowatt-hours used during the day. Use the electrical company's charge for each kilo-watt hour (likely between 6 and 10 cents) to determine the electrical cost for one day of school. You might do the same with your home and compare the daily electrical cost for your home with the daily cost for the school.

◆Answers

2. Meeting the challenge—Students observe a working tennis ball model and count the number of tennis balls (coulombs) entering the circuit for a period of 20 seconds. They then divide the number of tennis balls observed by 20 to determine the number of tennis balls entering each second (coulombs per second or amperes). Because each tennis ball (coulomb) is receiving 2 joules of energy (2 volts or 2 joules per coulomb), the energy entering the circuit each second is found by

multiplying the current (coulombs per second) and the voltage (joules per coulomb).

a and b. The answers will depend on the model used.

c. The answer will depend on the model used.

d. Because a watt is a joule per second, the number of watts is the same as the number of joules per second.

3a. When students learn the wattage of different household appliances, they may find it interesting to discover that their refrigerator runs on less wattage than their toaster.

b. If a television, or any other appliance, does not indicate the wattage, but does indicate the amperes, the number of amperes indicated multiplied by household voltage of 120 volts gives the wattage of the appliance. In the example, the television indicating 1.5 amperes would have a wattage of 180 watts (1.5 amperes × 120 volts).

MATERIALS AND SOURCES

Guide for Teachers

This section contains master lists (by module) of materials and equipment used in each activity, and gives addresses and phone numbers of suppliers of the few hard to find items used in the activities. Substitutions for some materials may be suggested in the "Preparation" section of each activity.

◆Module 1: Static Electricity

Master List of Materials for Each Group:

a metal spoon

a piece of silk cloth

a piece of flannel

a strip of Plexiglas (approximately 3 cm x 22 cm, see Activity 1)

a cylinder of paper (about a 3 cm x 20 cm strip rolled into a 6 cm diameter cylinder or hoop)

a meter stick

a wooden pencil

a piece of chalk

a large metal paper clip

two small, inflated balloons

a small piece of facial tissue

a quarter

a small piece of aluminum foil

a piece of string, about 60 cm long

a small foil flag tied to the end of a 30-cm piece of nylon thread (see Activity 4)

a plastic ruler or a piece of material (cardboard, stick) similar in size to a ruler (about 30 cm long)

regular size, metal paper clips

a piece of glass (test tube, glass rod, drinking glass)

a plastic cassette tape box

a piece of nylon stocking

a piece of plastic wrap

a half sheet of overhead projection material rolled to a diameter of about 2 cm and taped at the ends and middle

other materials that can be electrified such as: plastic wrap on the roll, transparent tape on the roll, etc. (see Activity 6)

a foil strip (1 cm x 10 cm) bent and hung on the end loop of a nylon thread (see Activity 9)

two approximately 11-cm-diameter aluminum foil pie pans

one large aluminum foil pie pan, 20 cm or so in diameter

two 1 cm x 4 cm pieces of regular weight (not heavy duty) aluminum foil

one clear glass container (drinking glass, jar, beaker) about 8 cm in diameter and at least 12 cm tall

two rubber bands which fit across the diameters of the pie pan to form an "x."

a large piece of Plexiglas (about 20 cm square)

a Styrofoam cup

a cup of water

a wide container to catch water

The following may be used by the entire class or the teacher:

a marker

six strips of paper or thin cardboard (see Guide to Activity 5)

a fluorescent light bulb or tube (any size, even one that is burned out)

a couple pieces of aluminum foil (about 20 cm x 30 cm each)

a couple pieces of notebook paper

a roll of cellophane tape

a pair of scissors

at least 2.5 m of insulated wire (with about 3 cm of insulation removed from each end)

◆Module 2: Current Electricity

Master List of Materials for Each Group:

three #48 flashlight bulbs

two "D" batteries (dry cells)

six 20-cm pieces of wire (#22 plastic-coated wire with about 3 cm of insulation removed from both ends or #24 enamel-coated wire with about 3 cm of insulation scraped or sanded from both ends)

two battery holders (each a thick rubber band and two attached Fahnestock clips, see Activity 16)

three bulb holders for #48 bulbs (socket)

one piece of #24 enamel-coated wire with about 4 cm of enamel scraped or sanded from each end, see Activity 17

assorted conducting and nonconducting materials (pencil "lead," metal paper clip, piece of paper, mylar), see Activity 17

assorted materials for building switches: poster board, paper clips, transparent tape, brass fasteners, aluminum foil, rubber bands, etc. See Activity 18

a #2 pencil sharpened at both ends with one cm of "lead" exposed at the middle, see Activity 19

an optional piece of #32 nichrome wire, about 1 or 1.5 m long

two switches, each made from a 5 cm x 5 cm piece of thin cardboard and two metal paper clips, see Activity 21

The following may be used by the entire class or the teacher:

two 2.5-m sections of grooved wooden or metal strips, see Activity 22

six tennis balls

a watch or clock that measures seconds

a slider made from a 10 cm x 46 cm piece of manila folder, see Activity 23

two old socks, each with the toe end cut off

Suppliers

The following suppliers are possible sources of materials which may be difficult to locate (Fahnestock clips (for the battery holders), sockets (bulb holders), and Van de Graaff machines). Not all materials are available from all suppliers.

Carolina Biological Supply Company
2700 York Road
Burlington, NC 27215
(919) 584-0381
(800) 334-5551
(800) 632-1231 (NC residents)
FAX (919) 584-3399

Carolina Biological Supply Company
Powell Laboratories Division
19355 McLoughlin Boulevard
Gladstone, OR 97027
(503) 656-1641
(800) 547-1733
FAX (503) 656-4208

Delta Education Inc.
P. O. Box 950
Hudson, NH 03051-9924
(800) 442-5444
FAX (603) 595-8580

Nasco
P. O. Box 901
Fort Atkinson, WI 53538
(800) 558-9595
(414) 563-2446

Nasco West
1524 Princeton Ave.
Modesto, CA 95352
(800) 558-9595
(209) 529-6957